FOOD AID AND INTERNATIONAL ECONOMIC GROWTH

UMA K. SRIVASTAVA
EARL O. HEADY
KEITH D. ROGERS
LEO V. MAYER

Food Aid
and
International
Economic
Growth

The Iowa State University Press
AMES, IOWA

This project was partly financed by the
United States Agency for International Development
AID/csd-2163

UMA K. SRIVASTAVA is Assistant Professor, Indian Institute of Management, Vastrapur, India.

EARL O. HEADY is Charles F. Curtiss Distinguished Professor of Agriculture, Professor of Economics, and Director of the Center for Agricultural and Rural Development, Iowa State University.

KEITH D. ROGERS is Staff Economist of the Center for Agricultural and Rural Development, Iowa State University, and is Chief-of-Party for the ISU-AID Sector Analysis Project in Thailand.

LEO V. MAYER is Agricultural Economist, Library of Congress, Washington, D.C.

Library of Congress Cataloging in Publication Data
Main entry under title:

Food aid and international economic growth.

    Bibliography: p.
    Includes index.
    1. Surplus agricultural commodities, American.
2. Food relief, American. 3. Counterpart funds.
4. Economic development. I. Srivastava, Uma K.
HD9006.F57   338.91′172′4073   74–23615
ISBN 0–8138–0640–2

CONTENTS

v

PREFACE

THE BALANCE between world food supplies and demands has fluctuated widely over several decades. Immediately following World War II, birthrates and life expectancies soared rapidly in both developed and undeveloped countries. With war-inflicted damages to agricultural production capacity spread widely over Europe, food was in short supply and its price was high. These circumstances created long-lasting world food shortages, and the United States geared up to meet these "seller's markets." However, by the mid-1950s world agricultural production not only had rebounded from war-burdened conditions but also was increasing relative to export markets. At this time the United States initiated farm policies to curtail domestic food production. As a result of production control programs (which were only partly effective) and high government support prices, stocks of major commodities began to accumulate on an interyear basis and had reached very large proportions by the early 1960s. In order to curtail surpluses and decrease stocks, the United States began a more vigorous domestic supply control program and embarked on a worldwide food aid activity. During the poor weather and crop shortfalls in 1966–67 and with rapid increases in world population in sight, world food market conditions improved; many experts predicted that the time of food surpluses in developed countries had ended. The United States relaxed its supply controls at that time. However, by 1968–69 weather conditions had improved and even less-developed countries were able to make substantial gains in their agriculture. But the long-expected world market rally did not materialize, and the United States once again had to screw down its production control mechanisms at an enlarged treasury cost. Again in 1972–73 parts of the world had unfavorable weather, and heavy export demands became the windfall of surplus-producing countries such as the United States. By 1973–74 experts were again predicting that a new era in world agricultural demand was in sight and never again would supply control and food aid programs be needed. By late 1974, however, the balance between world food supplies and demands seemed to be "normalizing," and some characteristics of old markets may be returning.

Food aid was a means for the United States to extend a humanitarian hand to less developed countries and also ease its own surplus problems from the late 1950s to the early 1970s. It is possible that these supply conditions could again arise. During the period in which U.S. food aid was at its height, its role in development gave rise to complex de-

vii

bates. Some analysts proposed that through market effects it dampened agricultural development of the low-income countries. Others argued that in terms of total societies, with special consideration of consumers, the net effect of food aid under the conditions it was extended had to be positive.

The study reported in this book was made to better quantify the effects of previous food aid programs on development, producer and consumer welfare, agricultural progress, and fiscal structures in recipient countries. Analysis is made of conditions under which consumer welfare can be enhanced and farmers can be insulated from negative price impacts. The reference country is India. The study was made at the invitation and under the financing of the United States Agency for International Development. The results contained herein are only part of those forthcoming from the cooperative project carried out in the Center for Agricultural and Rural Development of Iowa State University.

FOOD AID AND INTERNATIONAL ECONOMIC GROWTH

Dimensions of Food Aid

F O O D supplied under Public Law 480 (P.L. 480) to developing countries has been an important dimension of U.S. international economic aid since the mid-1950s. Food aid has helped accelerate the process of development in recipient countries in two significant ways: (1) it has reduced or eliminated the need to divert scarce foreign exchange resources from the importation of strategic capital goods and raw materials, and (2) it has eliminated the necessity of raising prices and rationing to minimize increases in food demand.[1] Although the idea of food aid originated from the difficulties in maintaining farm prices and incomes in the United States, the economic situation in the developing countries presented the possibility for transforming the surplus food into a useful tool of economic development in those countries. The effectiveness of this tool has varied from country to country depending on the intensity of food gap, the integration of food aid into the economic system, and the terms on which food aid was supplied.

Despite the growth-promoting effects of P.L. 480 food, this form of aid has become subject to criticism over the years on two counts: one set of critics has emphasized the effect of food aid in depressing prices and dampening incentives for producers in the recipient countries; the second set has stressed the inflationary implications of the accumulation and disbursement of counterpart funds arising from food aid.

The nature and composition of food aid have undergone various changes over the years, but the mutual interests of donor and recipient countries have motivated an uninterrupted flow. The United States, a major donor of food aid, has continued to be faced with structural disequilibrium in the agricultural sector. The U.S. commitment to prevent price and income depression in agriculture has resulted in excess accumulation of stocks, while recipient countries have been continuously faced with a lagging agricultural supply and expanding demand for agricultural products arising out of increased incomes and population growth.

However, the outlook for food aid in both donor and recipient countries has changed considerably. Surplus stocks have reached more moderate levels in the United States since the mid-1960s. With the decline in the surplus stocks has come a hardening of terms of U.S. food aid to recipient countries. More and more recipient countries are now required to make payments in dollars instead of local currencies. This requirement has radically altered the initial idea behind food aid, which was to augment total inflow of resources to developing countries without adding to international indebtedness and without affecting the future inflow of aid. The recipient countries, particularly in Asia, have experienced a perceptible technological transformation of agriculture in recent years which has led to a rapid increase in agricultural output. Under these circumstances the usefulness of food aid as a tool of economic development needs a fresh look in the next one or two decades.

P.L. 480

Evolution. The U.S. government has financed surplus disposal activities for selected agricultural commodities through various support and promotional programs for nearly four decades. Prior to 1954 surplus disposal activities were conducted under a number of independent authorizations. Since 1954 most disposal activities have been coordinated under the Agricultural Trade Development and Assistance Act, known as Public Law 480. The concepts and experiences with previous disposal activities were directly reflected in the provisions of P.L. 480. The logic of P.L. 480 was based on the assumption that countries with U.S. dollars would prefer to spend them on purchases of capital goods, and countries without U.S. dollars would be willing to purchase U.S. surplus agricultural commodities with their local currencies.

When P.L. 480 was enacted, it contained three titles or major provisions. Title I authorized the Commodity Credit Corporation (CCC) to finance the sale of $700 million of surplus farm commodities to foreign countries for local or "soft" currency of that country instead of U.S. dollars. The soft currency section of P.L. 480 drew on the experiences of the Marshall Plan and Mutual Security Act programs and retained the Mutual Security Act provision of depositing soft currency to an account for the U.S. Treasury. Title II extended CCC authority, as granted under the Mutual Security Act of 1953, to donate up to $300 million of surplus agricultural commodities from CCC stocks to relieve famine and other food emergencies overseas. The donation section of P.L. 480 incorporated the broad concept of famine relief and related to previous experience in attempting to expand effective purchasing power of the needy through food stamp and other related plans. Title III drew on the previous authorization of Section 416 and provided for donations to the needy at home and abroad, and the barter provisions from the CCC chapter were incorporated into the new act. In both cases the previous provisions were broadened and expanded to provide more extensive coverage.

The basic provisions of P.L. 480 have been extended repeatedly since enactment in 1954, and numerous changes have expanded the scope of the program. The 1956 extension (P.L. 540) permitted the CCC to pay costs of ocean freight for Title II and III agreements and authorized the appointment of a surplus disposal administrator within the United States Department of Agriculture (USDA) to coordinate P.L. 480 activities. The 1957 amendment (P.L. 128) softened the restriction on "friendly" nations to permit barter agreements and voluntary agency programs such as Cooperative for American Relief Everywhere (CARE) to use donations in Soviet satellite nations. The Cooley amendment provided for up to 25% of soft currency acquired under Title I to be provided as loans to U.S. or foreign firms to develop expanded markets for American products overseas (hereafter referred to as Cooley loans). The 1958 extension (P.L. 391) reduced restrictions on barter agreements by abolishing requirements of proof that the agreement was not replacing cash purchases of the commodity involved, and provided that barter agreements could be made with any free country as long as U.S. dollar sales were not disrupted.

The 1959 extension (P.L. 341) contained the first structural change in the 1954 act. Title IV was added to provide for long-term, low-interest credit sales of surplus commodities, with repayment being made in U.S. dollars over a period up to twenty years. Although numerous amendments and extensions were added to the original act, the objectives remained basically the same throughout the 1950s. Despite the fact that the original act carried a "Trade Development and Assistance" title, the purpose continued to be disposal of U.S. surpluses. From 1957 to 1960, however, there were indications that the objectives or goals of P.L. 480 were beginning to shift away from primary emphasis on surplus disposal toward new emphasis on foreign economic development. During this period increasing amounts of local currency were designated for development loans and grants. The support for more extensive concentration on economic development had reached a level that apparently forced a movement in that direction. A major change in policy was implemented through a four-year contract with India with a granting back of 40% of the local currency to be used for development. The extended contract periods provided for improved planning and implementation of development programs.

The 1961 extension of P.L. 480 (P.L. 92) included a permanent amendment to permit food grants to be used for economic development instead of being restricted to famine or emergency relief. Drawing on U.S. experience with school lunch programs, the 1962 Food and Agriculture Act (P.L. 703) amended Title III to provide for donations to be used in nonprofit school lunch programs in the recipient countries. Title IV was modified to provide for agreements between foreign and U.S. private firms under extended dollar credit terms. The 1964 extension and amendment (P.L. 638) restricted payment of freight equal only to the amount of the differential resulting from required transportation on U.S. ships. Proposed uses of Title I soft currency for grants or loans were subjected to approval of the House and Senate committees on agriculture. The 25% limit on funds for Cooley loans was removed, and Title III commodities were approved for self-help projects designed to alleviate the need for food aid.

The 1966 amendment (P.L. 808) officially changed the title of the program to Food for Peace and declared the purposes of the act as: promotion of international trade in agricultural commodities, combating hunger and malnutrition, furthering economic development, and implementing other programs. The noticeable absence of reference to surplus disposal reflected a change in the attitude prevailing in program execution during the early 1960s. Increased emphasis centered on helping those nations to help themselves. A second major change required transition to sales for dollars "whenever possible" by the end of 1967, and strictly to dollar sales or terms allowing for conversion of soft currency to dollars by the end of December 1971.

The 1968 amendment (P.L. 436) extended Title I and Title II activities through December 1970 and for the first time authorized expenditure of sales proceeds to finance population control programs. "Not less than 5 percentum of the total sales proceeds received each year shall, if requested by the foreign country, be used for voluntary programs to control population growth."[2]

Administration of Programs. Administration of P.L. 480 operations is handled primarily by three government agencies and corresponding delegations of authority—the USDA with delegation to the CCC, the Department of State with delegation to United States Agency for International Development (USAID), and the director of Food for Peace as a special assistant to the President. Formally the agencies involved in P.L. 480 programming interact through the Interagency Staff Committee (ISC) to coordinate their activities. The ISC includes representatives from the Department of Agriculture, the Department of State, USAID, Bureau of the Budget, Department of Treasury, Department of Commerce, United States Information Agency, the Office of Emergency Planning, and the director of Food for Peace.

Sales under Title I are financed by letters of credit through the CCC and commercial trade channels. Although the bulk of the administrative responsibility for Title I programs is handled by USAID, there are two exceptions: (1) the director of Food for Peace is charged with responsibility for continuous supervision and coordination of the functions of that program, and (2) the Secretary of State is responsible for foreign policy aspects of the food aid program. The ISC is the main decision-making body for Title I operations, since it reviews all activities in an attempt to coordinate the operations of various agencies. Expenditures and disbursements of soft currency that accrues to the United States are handled through numerous agencies, as indicated in Table 1.1. In broad terms nearly half of the local currency is designated for U.S. uses or private enterprise. (A lower estimate is obtained if common defense and Cooley loans are not included as U.S. uses.)

Most of the administrative responsibility for Title II programs is handled by USAID after the USDA determines what commodities are

TABLE 1.1. Authorized Uses of Local Currency under Section 104, P.L. 480

Currency Use	Responsible Agency
Agricultural market development	Dept. of Agriculture
Supplemental stockpile	Office of Civil Defense Mobilization
Common defense	Depts. of State (AID) and Defense
Purchase of goods for other countries	Dept. of State (AID)
Grants for economic development	Dept. of State (AID)
Loans to private enterprise	Export-Import Bank of Washington
Payment of U.S. obligations	Any authorized U.S. government agency
Loans to foreign governments	Dept. of State (AID) and Development Loan Fund
International educational exchange	Dept. of State
Translation of books and periodicals	U.S. Information Agency
Scientific, medical, cultural, and educational activities	National Science Foundation, Dept. of State, and other agencies
Buildings for U.S. government use	Dept. of State
Trade fairs	U.S. Information Agency
Acquisition, indexing, and dissemination of foreign publications	Library of Congress
American educational institutions	Dept. of State
Workshops in American studies	Dept. of State
Purchase of nonfood items for emergency uses	Dept. of State (AID)
Audio-visual materials	Dept. of State and U.S. Information Agency
Sales of dollars for U.S. tourists	Not assigned

in surplus supply and available from CCC stocks; USAID supervises the implementation of requests, distribution of commodities, and auditing procedures for Title II emergency relief and economic development operations.

Responsibilities for Title III programs are divided between USAID and the USDA. The USDA is responsible for determining which commodities and quantities are available and for approving the requests for those commodities; USAID is responsible for evaluation, coordination, and approval of distributing agencies in the foreign countries and for administering U.S. overseas activities. The administration of Title IV programs is the same as Title I programs with one exception: the National Advisory Council determines the payment period and interest rate for each individual Title IV agreement.

Magnitude of Operations. From July 1, 1954, through December 31, 1968, nearly $17.6 billion worth of commodities were shipped under various P.L. 480 authorizations (Table 1.2). Commodities worth $70 million were shipped during the first six months ending in December 1954. As the program expanded, the volume and value of commodities shipped increased rapidly to a high of more than $1.6 billion for 1964 (Table 1.3). Subsequently the value of products shipped declined gradually to just under $1.2 billion in 1968. Title I sales for local currency accounted for 65.0% of $11.4 billion of the total shipments (Table 1.2). Donations on a government-to-government basis and to voluntary organizations under Title II accounted for the second largest portion—18.7% or $3.3 billion. Title III bartering and Title IV dollar sales were 9.7 and 6.6% of the total or $1.7 and $1.2 billion respectively (Table 1.2).

On a commodity basis, wheat and rye overshadowed all other shipment by making up $9.1 billion or 51.7% of all commodity shipments through 1968 (Table 1.2). Feed grains accounted for $1.8 billion (10.1%) and rice another $1.1 billion (6.0%). In combination the food and feed grains represented 67.8% of all shipments under P.L. 480 authorizations. Other classes supplying significant amounts were cotton at $2.0 billion, fats and oils at $1.5 billion, and dairy products at $1.4 billion.

Shipments of the six major commodity groups followed a similar pattern of distribution under the various titles (Table 1.2). These six groups are wheat and rye, feed grains, rice, cotton, tobacco, and fats and oils plus oil seeds and meal. Soft currency sales accounted for about 70% of the total value of shipments for each individual group; the re-

TABLE 1.2. Value of Farm Commodities Shipped (by commodity) under **P.L. 480, July 1, 1954–December 31, 1968** (in thousands of dollars)

Commodity	Foreign Currency Sales (I)	Long-term Dollar Sales (IV)	Government-to-Government Donations (II)	Voluntary Agency Donations (II)	Barter (III)	Total	Percent of Total
Wheat and rye	6,484,748	679,109	601,229	656,735	649,591	9,071,412	51.7
Feed grains	795,085	93,381	147,494	178,424	568,187	1,782,571	10.1
Rice	846,863	113,809	29,695	53,062	15,155	1,058,584	6.0
Cotton	1,519,938	158,217	15,267	…	299,808	1,993,230	11.3
Tobacco	362,285	27,196	…	…	126,196	515,677	2.9
Fats and oils	1,161,469	78,968	63,267	222,826	4,876	1,531,406	8.7
Oilseeds and meal	…	10,717	…	…	16,645	27,362	0.2
Dairy products	165,444	3,141	143,505	1,100,436	20,130	1,432,656	8.1
Meat and poultry	58,915	58	…	…	…	58,973	0.3
Fruits and vegetables	24,608	2,566	6,751	19,594	2,526	56,045	0.3
Other	4,220	…	5,330	46,623	7,029	63,202	0.4
Total	11,423,575	1,167,162	1,012,538	2,277,700	1,710,143	17,591,118	100.0
Percent of total	65.0	6.6	5.8	12.9	9.7	100.0	

Source: U.S. Congress, *Food for Peace*, House Document 104–91/1, p. 97.

TABLE 1.3. Value of Farm Commodities Shipped (by year) under P.L. 480, July 1, 1954–December 31, 1968 (in millions of dollars)

Calendar Year	Foreign Currency Sales (I)	Long-term Dollar Sales (IV)	Government-to-Government Donations (II)	Voluntary Agency Donations (II)	Barter (III)	Total	Total Agricultural Exports	Percent of Total
1954	...	...	28	20	22	70	1,585	4
1955	263	...	56	186	262	767	3,199	24
1956	638	...	65	187	372	1,262	4,170	30
1957	760	...	39	175	244	1,218	4,506	27
1958	752	...	43	159	65	1,019	3,855	26
1959	731	...	32	111	175	1,049	3,955	27
1960	1,014	...	49	124	117	1,304	4,832	27
1961	878	1	93	151	181	1,304	5,024	26
1962	1,007	42	81	178	137	1,445	5,034	29
1963	1,162	52	99	160	38	1,511	5,584	27
1964	1,232	97	62	186	35	1,612	6,348	25
1965	899	152	73	180	5	1,309	6,229	21
1966	815	239	79	132	41	1,306	6,881	19
1967	736	201	108	179	13	1,237	6,383	19
1968	539	385	101	150	3	1,178	6,228	19
Total	11,426	1,169	1,008	2,278	1,710	17,591	73,813	24

Source: U.S. Congress, *Food for Peace*, House Document 104–91/1, p. 109.

maining titles each accounted for 15% or less than 45% of the total, while barter agreements were about 32% under Title III. Soft currency sales of dairy products were just under 12%; donations to voluntary agencies for child feeding and related uses under Title II were about 78% of the total supplied.

Several structural changes have taken place in the program and are reflected in the financing. Reaction to criticism from foreign competitors in the late 1950s that the U.S. barter program was disrupting normal trade brought about a decline in the barter program from a high of $372 million in 1956 to $3.0 million in 1968 (Table 1.3). Donations to voluntary agencies reached a high of $186 million in 1964. The government-to-government portion of Title II programs is providing approximately $250 million of commodities annually. Dollar sales under Title IV began in 1961 and have increased steadily in line with the transition to sales for dollars only since December 1971. Although dollar sales have increased, they have not increased as fast as soft currency sales have declined. Consequently, total sales hit a high of $1.3 billion in 1964 and have declined annually to $0.9 billion in 1968 (Table 1.3).

Shifts in geographic concentration of the P.L. 480 program have taken place and are reflected in the comparison of 1968 contracts with totals for the program from its inception. Although the Near East–South Asia area continues to be a major recipient of sales agreements, that part of the world no longer dominates the sales as it did in earlier years when it accounted for 56.1% of the total, with Europe and the Far East–Pacific regions accounting for less than 20% each (Table 1.4). The 1968 contracts reflect negligible sales to Europe, a decline to 37.4% for the Near East–South Asia area, an increase to 39.8% for the Far East–Pacific area, and increases of about 5% each for Africa and Latin America.

Donations under Title II appear to have shifted from nearly equal distribution among Africa (23.2%), Near East–South Asia area (28.3%), and Far East–Pacific area (22.3%) to the Far East–Pacific area where almost 58% of the donations were made in 1968 (Table 1.4). Donations to the European area fell to zero in 1968, while contributions to the World Food Program nearly doubled to 13.7%. The barter program under Title III probably reflects the most noticeable shifts: Europe received 61.7% of the barter commodities in the past but only 7.0% in 1968; the Near East and Far East areas previously received 9.5 and 15.4% respectively and accounted for 28.5 and 60.8% in 1968.

Changes in allocation of foreign currency and donated commodities also provide an indication of the changing emphasis of the P.L.

TABLE 1.4. Destination of P.L. 480 Commodities by Agreement

Destination	1954 through 1968		1968 Contract	
	Value[a] ($ million)	Percent	Value[a] ($ million)	Percent
Title I				
Europe	3,101.6	16.6	2.2	0.3
Africa	602.8	3.2	62.7	8.1
Near East–South Asia	10,440.8	56.1	290.3	37.4
Far East–Pacific	2,932.7	15.7	309.5	39.8
Latin America	1,567.0	8.4	111.5	14.4
Total	18,644.9	100.0	776.2	100.0
Title II				
Europe	190.0	8.5	0	0
Africa	519.8	23.2	14.3	9.2
Near East–South Asia	636.7	28.3	21.1	13.6
Far East–Pacific	500.0	22.3	89.3	57.6
Latin America	186.1	8.3	9.1	5.9
World Food Program	183.2	8.2	21.3	13.7
Other	26.2	1.2	0	0
Total	2,242.0	100.0	155.0	100.0
Title III				
Europe	1,053.2	61.7	0.2	7.0
Africa	54.9	3.2	. . .[b]	. . .[b]
Near East–South Asia	163.3	9.5	0.8	28.5
Far East–Pacific	263.5	15.4	1.7	60.8
North America	3.5	0.2	0	0
Latin America	171.7	10.0	0.1	3.6
Total	1,710.0	100.0	2.8	100.0

Source: U.S. Congress, *Food for Peace*, House Document No. 104–91/1, pp. 112–61.
a. C.C.C. cost including ocean transportation.
b. Negligible.

480 program. From 1954 to 1968 more than 70% of the funds resulting from soft currency sales were allocated for foreign government loans and U.S. uses (Table 1.5). Common defense used almost 11%, and a little over 14% was released to the recipient governments as grants for economic development. In 1968 a third of the soft currency released went for foreign government loans. The U.S. uses represented less than 17%, and grants for economic development fell to less than 2% of total funds used. Emphasis of 1968 donation programs under Title II were similar to the historic patterns of donations. Disaster relief accounted for about 50% of the donations, economic development for 25–30%, and refugee and child feeding programs around 10% each.

Over the years P.L. 480 has accounted for a significant portion of U.S. commodity exports. In 1956 P.L. 480 exports amounted to 30% of all agricultural exports from the United States. In 1958 and 1959 both P.L. 480 and commercial exports declined slightly, and P.L. 480

TABLE 1.5. Uses of Foreign Currency or Commodities by Agreement

	1954 through 1968		1968 Contract	
Purpose	Value ($ million)	Percent	Value ($ million)	Percent
Title I				
a. Common defense	1,330.6	10.9	85.6	32.6
b. Loans to private enterprise	533.3	4.4	11.4	4.3
c. Loans to foreign government	5,595.8	45.7	91.1	34.7
d. Grants for economic development	1,744.7	14.2	4.9	1.9
e. Grants for family welfare	41.8	0.3	23.3	8.9
f. Pest control	1.9	. . .ª	1.9	0.7
g. U.S. uses	3,007.4	24.5	44.6	16.9
Total	12,255.5	100.0	262.8	100.0
Title II				
a. Disaster relief	1,039.1	46.3	81.4	52.5
b. Child feeding	273.7	12.2	12.2	7.9
c. Refugees	217.3	9.7	18.2	11.7
d. Voluntary agencies	22.6	1.0	0	0
e. Economic development	662.8	29.6	43.2	27.9
f. Other	26.5	1.2	0	0
Total	2,242.0	100.0	155.0	100.0
Title III				
a. Voluntary agencies	3,243.6	100.0	152.1	100.0

Source: U.S. Congress, *Food for Peace*, House Document No. 104–91/1, pp. 126–57.
a. Negligible.

shipments represented 26–27% of the total. When commercial exports began to increase during the 1960s, P.L. 480 programs were expanded and continued to represent 25–27% of total exports (Table 1.6).

In 1965 P.L. 480 programs began to decline; with a rise in commercial exports through 1966, P.L. 480 shipments fell to 19% of the total. In 1967 and 1968 a decline in commercial exports coincided with a cutback in the P.L. 480 programs, and P.L. 480 shipments held constant at 19% of total exports. Over the entire period since 1954, 24% of U.S. agricultural exports have been handled under concessional terms of P.L. 480. Another 3% was exported under the Mutual Security Act, bringing the total government-sponsored exports up to 27%.

THEORETICAL BACKGROUND. The acceleration of economic growth in developing countries is designed to increase per capita incomes. Since the marginal propensity to consume and the income elasticity of demand are high in the initial stages, economic growth leads to a rapid rise in the demand for food, and the demand for

TABLE 1.6. **Value of Farm Commodities Shipped (by year) under P.L. 480 Compared with Total Exports of Farm Commodities, July 1, 1954–December 31, 1968 (in millions of dollars)**

Calendar Year	Total P.L. 480	Mutual Security	Total Gov't. Programs	Commercial Sales	Total Exports	P.L. 480 as Percent of Total
1954	70	211	281	1,304	1,585	4
1955	767	351	1,118	2,081	3,199	24
1956	1,262	449	1,711	2,459	4,170	30
1957	1,218	318	1,536	2,970	4,506	27
1958	1,019	214	1,233	2,622	3,855	26
1959	1,049	158	1,207	2,748	3,955	27
1960	1,304	157	1,461	3,371	4,832	27
1961	1,304	179	1,483	3,541	5,024	26
1962	1,445	35	1,480	3,554	5,034	29
1963	1,511	11	1,522	4,062	5,584	27
1964	1,612	23	1,635	4,713	6,348	25
1965	1,309	26	1,335	4,894	6,229	21
1966	1,306	47	1,353	5,528	6,881	19
1967	1,237	33	1,370	5,113	6,383	19
1968	1,178	11	1,189	5,039	6,228	19
Total	17,591	2,223	19,814	53,999	73,813	24

Source: U.S. Congress, *Food for Peace,* House Document No. 104–91/1, p. 97.

food increases with population growth. The relationship between demand for food, per capita income, and the rate of growth of population can be expressed as

$$d_r = \eta y_r + p_r \tag{1.1}$$

where

d = demand for food
y = per capita income
η = income elasticity of demand for food
p = population
r = rate of growth

To arrive at the aggregate demand for food at any point of time, d_t, (1.1) has to be multiplied by the initial level of food demand d_0:

$$d_t = (1 + \eta y_r + p_r)^t d_0 \tag{1.2}$$

Side by side with the increasing demand for food is the lagging supply from domestic sources in the initial stages of economic growth.

Restraints on supply include the lack of a conducive agrarian structure, pressure of population on land, and inadequacy of physical inputs and appropriate policies and capital. As a result the phenomenon of a food gap emerges. The food gap can be expressed as

$$g = (d_t - F_t) \qquad \text{(1.3a)}$$

where

$$g = \text{food gap}$$
$$F_t = \text{food supply in the period } t$$

Substituting (1.2) for d_t we get

$$g = (1 + \eta y_r + p_r)^t d_0 - F_t \qquad \text{(1.3b)}$$

and $g > 0$.

In a simplified case of a closed economy, the food gap acts as a constraint on the desired rate of growth, because domestically produced food is identical to the total food supply in the economy. In these circumstances an endeavor to achieve an otherwise feasible rate of growth will manifest itself by way of the value of the money income multiplier exceeding the value of the real income multiplier.[3] Consequently the excess monetary demand for goods and services, particularly food, would induce a food price inflation. In a realistic case of open economy, however, food gap may not necessarily become a constraint on the growth process, because two alternatives may be available to bridge the food gap: (1) imports through normal trade channels, and (2) inflow of foreign capital for purchases of food.

An open economy is a condition necessary but not sufficient for preventing the food gap from acquiring the form of a constraint on the growth process. The sufficiency condition will be fulfilled only if exports are large enough to meet the foreign exchange required for food imports over and above normal developmental imports. If exports fail to do this, the magnitude of foreign capital inflow must be large enough to meet the deficit arising in the current account due to the combined quantum of imports of capital goods, maintenance imports, and food imports.

To elaborate the sufficiency conditions it is important to bring out the nature of interactions among three major types of constraints on economic growth—food, foreign exchange, and savings. This analysis will highlight the relevance of the food constraint in the context of the growth process. First, let the economy be open on the current account only while it is still closed on the capital account. The current account comprises both exports and imports of goods and services (invisibles). The possibility of importing food for economic development depends on the magnitude of exports of goods and services in relation to the import requirements other than food. But a developing economy faces a problem of a minimum necessary quantum of foreign exchange resources for importing the strategic capital goods and maintenance equipment (raw material, spare parts, and the like) which are indispensable. Under these circumstances three possible situations of foreign exchange gap may exist:

$$G = (d_f + M) - E \gtrless 0 \tag{1.4}$$

where

$G =$ foreign exchange gap
$E =$ exports
$d_f =$ required foreign capital goods imports
$M =$ maintenance imports

In the developing countries (excluding oil-rich countries) the foreign exchange gap is positive; it is difficult for these countries to import the minimum necessary food without a reduction in the magnitude of foreign capital goods and/or maintenance imports. Such a reduction slows down the rate of growth itself, and the food gap becomes a constraint on the acceleration of the rate of growth.

Now let the economy be open on the capital account at the same time. Whether the food gap emerges as an additional constraint on the growth process will depend on the magnitude of the foreign capital inflow. Foreign capital inflow includes the inflow of long-term private capital and capital given in the form of aid. Foreign aid constitutes a major part of foreign capital inflow. From the Keynesian standpoint the rationale of foreign aid in economic growth is to bridge the savings gap, which can be written as

$$c_t = [K (y_r + p_r) - S] y_t \tag{1.5a}$$

Substituting the marginal savings rate for constant S we get

$$c_t = [K (y_r + p_r) - (a + by_r)] y_t \tag{1.5b}$$

where

c_t = foreign aid
K = capital output ratio
a = intercept term in the savings function
b = coefficient of the marginal savings rate

But from the modern standpoint, if the foreign exchange gap is larger than the savings gap, the foreign aid (c_t) has to be equal to the foreign exchange gap, because the inadequacy of strategic capital goods and raw materials (import content of investment) will make it difficult to use the entire amount of domestic savings.[4] In this case the Keynesian savings-income identity would hold on an ex post basis but not on an ex ante basis, and the need for foreign aid would continue to exist even if domestic savings equal investment—i.e., savings gap is zero.

A number of individuals and agencies have tried to work out foreign exchange and savings gaps for the developing countries.[5] The foreign exchange gap in all the estimates turns out to be larger than the savings gap. The actual foreign exchange inflow, however, has been much smaller than necessary on the basis of foreign exchange gap. In these circumstances even the maintenance of bare minimum food imports would have necessitated a diversion of scarce foreign exchange resources from the developmental requirements despite the availability of foreign aid. Food aid has bridged the food gap and helped accelerate economic growth in the recipient countries.

Economists have emphasized the fact that food aid is not a substitute for financial aid. If food aid is substituted for financial aid, the gains of food aid will be more than offset because food aid is considered inferior to financial aid. Schultz argues:

If these underdeveloped countries had a choice of receiving from the United States either dollars or farm products of equivalent value at world prices, they with few exceptions would have preferred to have the dollars, because the dollars would have been more to them in achieving economic growth or in serving other purposes that they ranked high among their national goals.[6]

Further, the flexibility of the use inherent in the very nature of untied dollar aid is almost missing in the committed surplus food aid.[7]

The role of food aid in the perspective of inflow of resources from developed to developing countries has been excellently summed up by a Food and Agriculture Organization (FAO) study:

While the food aid is inferior to aid given in the form of currency such as dollars, this does not necessarily imply that giving aid in this form is not useful, provided this aid is given for augmenting the investible resources for a development program. In the countries where the shortage of food is one of the main barriers to accelerated economic development, such aid properly conceived with respect to timing and magnitude may be just as important as other forms of aid.[8]

Food aid requirements have varied from country to country and at different times in the same country, depending on the income level.

INCOME LEVEL AND DEMAND FOR FOOD AID. The total quantity of food aid that can be used for a particular development project or program, the multiplier effect on income, and the derived demand for nonfood commodities all depend on the response of consumer groups providing labor for the development projects. Engel's law with respect to food consumption patterns states that the proportion of income spent on food declines as income rises. Food expenditures represent a high proportion of budget allocations at low budget levels and decrease at higher income levels. At low income levels the consumer survives on a minimum of all commodities, and a high percentage of the budget is used for food. As the budget increases, food consumption expands rapidly at first and begins to decline as an adequate nutritional level is approached. Food expenditures continue to increase but at a decreasing rate as proteins are substituted for carbohydrates and the physical limit for individual consumption is approached.[9]

Empirical Studies. The validity of Engel's law was verified by Houthakker in a cross-sectional study of personal expenditure patterns using international data.[10] Although the Houthakker study reports total expenditure instead of income (which is used in the strict formulation of the law), the results confirm the more rigorous formulation of Engel's law.[11] Using data published by Houthakker, we have attempted to develop an international Engel curve for food.

We considered three functional forms: (1) the percentage of budget spent for food on total expenditures, (2) the percentage of budget spent for food on the log of total expenditures, and (3) the log of percentage of budget spent for food on the log of total expenditures.[12] The semilog function displayed in Figure 1.1 resulted in the best fit (R^2 for semilog $= 0.68$, R^2 for linear functions $= 0.63$, and R^2 for double-log functions $= 0.65$). Values on the estimated Engel curve range from a high of 100% at the very low budget levels down to approximately 35% of a total annual per capita expenditure of \$2,500. At the low budget level the proportion spent on food decreases rapidly as expend-

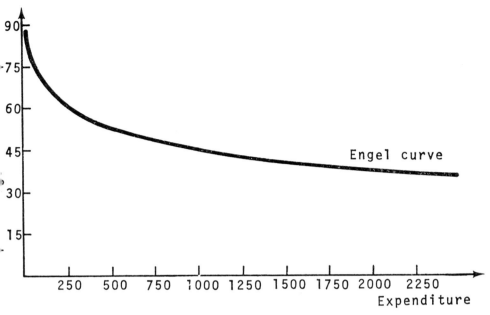

Fig. 1.1. Estimated international Engel curve for food consumption based on a semilog function.

iture increases up to about $750 where the slope of the function begins to stabilize.

Mellor argues that because tastes and preferences differ so widely between countries, comparisons of international data are not likely to be useful for detailed studies.[13] He agrees, however, that for broad aggregates of commodities, the international comparisons provide estimates surprisingly close to those from intracountry cross-sectional studies. Similarly, Stevens has stated that "international comparisons of Engel curve data provide more convincing evidence on the general magnitude of the income elasticity of total food during development."[14]

In a recent study of food consumption by the National Council of Applied Economic Research of New Delhi, the data indicate that the average yearly expenditure of an Indian consumer was $67.36: 52.5% was spent on food, 7.0% on clothing, 5.9% on fuel and light, and 34.6% on other items (Table 1.7).[15] Expenditures ranged from less than Rs 106.8 (about $22) to more than Rs 672 (about $140); food expenditures

TABLE 1.7. Average per Capita Expenditure per Month and Year in India

Commodity Group	Per Month (Rs)	Per Year (Rs)	($)[a]	Percent
Food	14.11	169.32	35.39	52.5
Fuel and light	1.58	18.96	3.96	5.9
Clothing	1.88	22.56	4.71	7.0
Other	9.29	111.48	23.30	34.6
Total	26.86	322.32	67.36	100.0

Source: National Council of Applied Economic Research, *All-India Consumer Expenditure Survey*, p. 49.
   a. Official exchange rate for period covered by the study, 1964 and 1965, averaged: $1 = Rs 4.785.

ranged from 65% down to 30%. Income elasticity of demand was estimated for wheat at 0.58 and for rice at 0.47. The elasticity for all cereals was estimated at 0.27; maize, jowar, and small millet had negative coefficients. Monthly per capita food expenditure in India (by income classes) is presented in Table 1.8.

In a similar study of food consumption in Korea for 1964–67, income elasticity for grain was estimated at 0.55 and for all food at 0.54 (Table 1.9).[16] Total per capita expenditure in the Korean study ranged from $58 to $125 with an $80 average. The range of percentage of expenditure for food was from 79 down to 54 with an average of 65.6.

TABLE 1.8. Monthly per Capita Food Expenditure in India

Income Class (Rs)	Total Expenditure (RS)	Total Food (Rs)	($)[a]	Percent
Under 8.9	11.57	7.49	1.57	64.8
9.0–11.9	14.64	9.02	1.89	61.6
12.0–13.9	18.52	10.37	2.17	56.0
14.0–15.9	18.08	10.98	2.29	60.8
16.0–18.9	24.55	13.52	2.83	55.1
19.0–21.9	22.45	12.77	2.67	56.9
22.0–24.9	29.50	16.07	3.36	54.6
25.0–28.9	. . .[b]	. . .[b]	. . .[b]	. . .[b]
29.0–34.9	33.80	15.96	3.34	47.3
35.0–43.9	37.01	17.91	3.74	48.4
44.0–55.9	51.30	23.49	4.91	45.8
Over 56.0	99.84	29.77	6.22	29.8
Average	26.86	14.11	2.95	52.5

Source: National Council of Applied Economic Research, *All-India Consumer Expenditure Survey*, pp. 118–19.
   a. Official exchange rate: $1 = Rs 4.785.
   b. Data inconsistent due to reporting of unusual wedding expenditures.

TABLE 1.9. Food Expenditure in Korea per Household by Income Class

Income Class (in 1,000 Won)	No. per House-hold	Total Expenditure (Won)[a]	Total Food		Percent
			(Won)	($)[b]	
Under 72	4.2	60,767	48,220	189.10	79.3
72– 96	5.3	85,022	63,810	250.02	75.0
96–120	5.6	107,235	76,642	300.56	71.5
120–144	6.5	132,528	87,350	342.55	65.0
144–168	7.3	156,193	97,677	383.05	62.6
168–192	6.9	180,221	106,395	417.24	59.0
Over 192	7.9	249,100	133,916	525.16	53.8
Average	6.0	123,934	81,307	318.85	65.6

Source: Ki Hyuk Pak and Kee Chun Hau, *An Analysis of Food Consumption in the Republic of Korea*, p. 81.
 a. Unit is 1964 Won.
 b. Official exchange rate: $1 = Won 255.

In summarizing several studies by FAO, Goreux estimates the income elasticity of food demand to be 0.85 at an annual per capita income of $50 and 0.25 at $1,500.[17] Coale and Hoover cite Palvia's estimate of the elasticity of demand for food at 0.8 in India relating to the period up to 1971.[18] In an analysis of international data from 35 countries, Stevens estimated the elasticity at about 0.8 at $50 and about 0.6 at $1,000. In a similar analysis of data from 13 countries, Stevens obtained estimates of 0.8 and 0.56 at low ($75) and high ($600) income levels respectively.[19] Analyzing data published in a study by Kuznets, Stevens estimated the elasticity coefficient at 0.75 with a double-log function.[20] Mellor suggests that the appropriate elasticities for developing countries range from 0.9 at low income levels down to 0.5 at high income levels.[21] Elsewhere Johnston and Mellor estimate that the elasticity is 0.6 or higher in developing countries.[22]

Results of these studies are summarized in Figure 1.2 by plotting the elasticity estimates against consumption expenditure on a semilog scale.[23] Over the range from $74 to $600 the estimates are bounded by data from Houthakker at the upper limit and from Goreux at the lower limit. At low income levels (below $100) the estimates are quite close, with the spread increasing at high income levels.

To analyze the impact of consumption behavior at different income levels on the generation of effective demand for food and economic development, we selected three levels as representative of the conditions under which food aid is programmed. The three levels of annual per capita income examined in detail are $75 as representative of

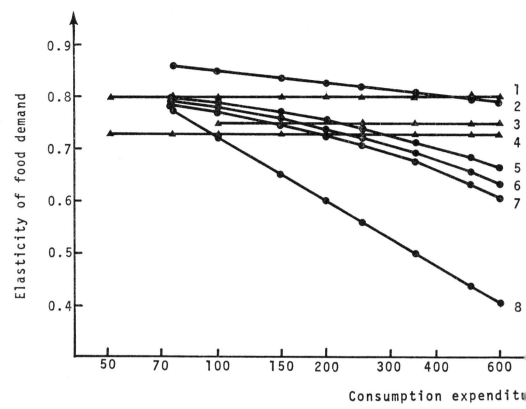

Fig. 1.2. Income elasticity estimates.

Sources: (1) Palvia by Coale and Hoover, op. cit.,
          (2) Houthakker, op. cit.,
          (3) Stevens, op. cit.,
          (4) Pak and Hau, op. cit.,
          (5) Goreux, op. cit.

low, $250 representing medium, and $450 representing high. While
P.L. 480 contracts were authorized for 37 countries during calendar year
1968, approximately 70% of the food was contracted by countries with
per capita incomes of $50–100 per year (Table 1.10). Another 21%
was contracted by countries of over $300.

LOW INCOME RECIPIENTS. Countries receiving food aid that have annual
per capita income close to $75 include the Congo ($87), Kenya
($100), Niger ($73), Nigeria ($68), Sierra Leone ($111), Somali
($62), Afghanistan ($52), and South Viet Nam ($108). Most other

TABLE 1.10.   Percentage of 1968 Food Aid Contracted by Recipient Country per Capita Expenditure Level

Expenditure in Dollars	Percentage of Food Aid	Cumulative Percentage
50– 74	18.64	18.64
75– 99	50.61	69.25
100–149	10.10	79.35
150–199	8.64	87.99
200–299	2.95	90.99
300–399	2.80	93.74
400–499	0.44	94.18
Other	5.82	100.00

Source: U.S. Congress, *Food for Peace,* House Document 104–91/1.

countries of the world have segments of the population with similar income levels, so the following discussion is applicable to low income strata within countries as well as to countries with similar averages.

The analysis is based on the premise that the recipient country finances part of a development project or program through the use of food aid. For example, consider an irrigation project that requires 100 units of investment to construct a reservoir and irrigation canals to increase agricultural production. We assume that the project inputs consist of 70% direct labor, 20% goods and services purchased locally, and 10% imported materials and equipment. How much of the cost can be financed with food aid?

The labor needed for the project will increase employment and income directly by 70 units. Each worker will increase his consumption of food and other consumer goods depending on his level of income elasticity. On the basis of the studies summarized earlier, low income consumers are estimated to have an income elasticity of demand for food of approximately 0.8. At $75 the average propensity to consume food was estimated at 0.55 for the Indian data, 0.62 for the USDA study, 0.73 by the Houthakker data, and 0.78 with Korean data, for a mean value ranging between 0.67–0.70. Comprehensive estimates of the food proportion of total consumer expenditures are quite limited. The United Nations has estimated per capita income of 101 countries of the world but has estimated food consumption for only 17 countries. The plot of the 17-country estimates in Figure 1.3 with the Engel curve estimated by Stevens indicates that the small sample is not sufficient to improve on earlier estimates of the Engel curve.[24] Only half the countries fall within the area outlined by the broken lines identifying points 10% above or below the estimated Engel curve at each income level.

For the average low income consumer, part of the income re-

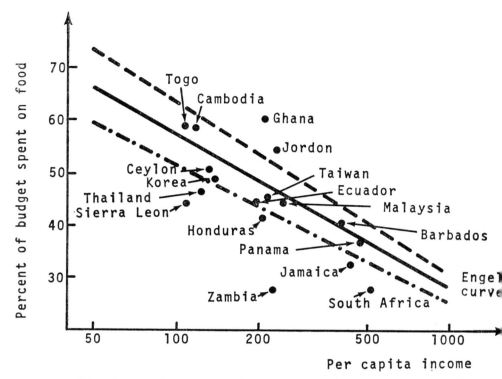

Fig. 1.3. International comparison of proportion of consumer budget spent on food.

ceived from wages will be saved, part will be used to pay taxes, and part will be used to purchase consumer goods. Most of the consumer demand will be for domestically produced goods, but a small portion will be for imported consumer goods. Ezekiel estimates that at the margin, savings equal about 9% of additional income.[25]

Deducting the 26% for savings (6.3 units), taxes (6.3 units), and imports (5.6 units), about 51.8 of the 70 units paid for wages will be left to purchase domestic goods and services. In combination an estimated elasticity of 0.8 and an average propensity to consume food of 0.67–0.70 imply a marginal propensity to consume food of about 0.55. (Since elasticity is equal to marginal propensity to consume divided by average propensity to consume, it follows that marginal propensity to consume is equal to average propensity to consume times elasticity.) If 55% of the increase in income after savings, taxes, and imports is spent on food, the 70 units of investment used for wages will generate a demand for 28.5 units of food. However, part of the food price represents marketing costs, so only part of the 28.5 units represents increased demand for actual food commodities. Ezekiel estimates that the marketing costs for food are 15% in rural areas where food is sold at retail in about the same form it comes from the farmer.[26] Deducting the 15% representing domestic services, the actual food demand would equal about 24.2 units. If surplus commodities could be matched with the native diet, 24.2 units of food could be supplied directly to the workers as wages-in-kind or indirectly through a price-controlled shop without affecting aggregate demand for or supply of domestic food. At this level food aid could be used to finance only one-fourth of the cost of the project. If in contrast 100 units of food were sold on the market and the income used to finance the project, a net increase in demand of 24 units implies that 76 units of the food would replace demand for domestic commodities. Before drawing a conclusion, it is necessary to consider what happens to the other 30 units of expenditure (20 for goods and services and 10 for imports).

The 10 units used to import materials and equipment are paid to the exporting country and leave the economy of the recipient country. The remaining 20 units are paid to domestic producers for goods and services. If there is excess capacity for supplying nonfood goods and services, a larger quantity can be sold at the same price. If supply is limited, the price will be bid up. In either case domestic producers receive additional income in the amount of 20 units.

Again part of the additional income will be saved, part will be used to pay taxes, and part will be used to purchase consumer goods or additional raw materials for future production. Deducting the 26% for savings (1.8 units), taxes (1.8 units), and imports (1.6 units), 14.8 units are left as disposable income to be spent on domestic consumer goods.

With a marginal propensity to consume food of 0.55, 8.1 units will be spent for food. Deducting the 15% for marketing services, 6.9 units will represent additional demand for food and the remaining 1.2 units for services. Adding the demand generated from the direct purchase of domestic goods and services to the demand generated from wages, the first-round increase in demand would be 31.3 units of food and 35.5 units of nonfood goods and services (Table 1.11).

In the second round 26.2 of the 35.5 units of income to domestic producers will be available as disposable income after deducting savings (3.2), taxes (3.2), and imports (2.8); 14.4 units will be spent for food and 11.8 units for nonfood (Table 1.11). Deducting the marketing costs on

TABLE 1.11. Aggregate Impact of 100 Units of Investment on Selected Economic Variables in Low Income Countries

Round	Gross Domestic Income	Savings	Taxes	Imports	Disposable Income	Derived Demand		
						Retail food	Wholesale food	Goods and services
1 (wages)[a]	70.00	6.30	6.30	5.60	51.80	28.49	24.22	27.58
(other)[b]	20.00	1.80	1.80	1.60	14.80	8.14	6.92	7.88
2	35.46	.19	3.19	2.84	26.24	14.43	12.27	13.97
3	13.97	1.26	1.26	1.12	10.34	5.69	4.83	5.50
4	5.50	.50	.50	.44	4.07	2.23	1.90	2.17
5	2.17	.20	.20	.17	1.61	.88	.75	.86
6	.86	.08	.08	.07	.64	.35	.30	.34
7	.34	.03	.03	.03	.25	.14	.12	.13
8	.13	.01	.01	.01	.10	.05	.04	.05
9	.05	.00	.00	.00	.04	.02	.02	.02
10	.02	.00	.00	.00	.01	.01	.01	.00
Total	148.50	13.37	13.37	11.88	109.90	60.43	51.38	58.50

Statistics: Savings = 9%, taxes = 9%, imports = 8%, marginal propensity to consume food = 0.55, marketing costs = 15%.
a. First-round impact of project expenditures directly for wages.
b. First-round impact of project expenditures for domestic goods and services.

food, 12.3 units of food will be demanded in the second round and 14.0 units of nonfood and services. Adding the first round to the second round brings the total food demand generated by the project to 43.4 units.

Expanding the analysis through ten rounds exhausts the multiplier effect of spending and responding with the assumed coefficients. Theoretically the total increase in income reaches 148.5 units and derived demand for food reaches 51.4 units as the result of the original investment of 100 units.

In the multiplier analysis, total expansion of the spending and responding is limited by the "leakage" out of consumers' hands. The usual leakage results from savings, taxes, and imports. The income multiplier is defined as $\dfrac{1}{s + g + m}$ where s, g, and m represent marginal savings, taxation, and import rates. The larger the sum of these three variables, the greater the leakage during each round and consequently the lower the multiplier effect. Using 26% as the estimated sum of s, g, and m implies a Keynesian investment-income multiplier of 3.85, which should produce 385 units of income from 100 units of investment supplied from domestic sources. However, at each round it was implicitly assumed that the food demand would be satisfied with surplus food aid, which also represents an import and further reduces the income to domestic producers at each round.

Under an assumption of four months for the income-expenditure lag, 94% of the increase in income and food demand would occur during the first year; under an assumption of three months for the lag, over 97.5% of the increase occurs during the first year. In either case the increases in income and demand for food occur rapidly in the low income countries due to to the high proportion of the budget allocated to food demand and consequently the rapid leakage from the economy when food aid is used to meet increased demands. Under these conditions about 50 units or half of the original investment could be financed in the first year through the use of food aid without affecting the domestic market prices.

In addition to the multiplier effect on income and food demand, the project would generate 12.5–13.0 units of savings and a similar amount of tax revenue in the first 12–15 months. Presumably the increase in savings would be channeled into investment and would increase productivity in future periods. Using a multiplier of the magnitude determined above (1.39 for three rounds), the 13 units of savings would generate 18 units of additional income in the second year and another 6.2 units of demand for food, bringing the total food demand for two years (six rounds) to 57.4 units. To balance supply with demand, 48.2 units of the surplus food should be supplied in the first year and the remaining 9.2 units in the second year.

The method used to pay the workers (cash, coupons, wages-in-kind, etc.) for the portion of their income that will be spent on food is immaterial if the supply of food aid is matched with the increased demand resulting from the investment. Paying wages and then recapturing the revenue from food sales is simply a balancing transaction and does not generate revenue for the government any more than issuing food coupons or wages-in-kind.

MEDIUM INCOME RECIPIENTS. The second group of developing countries considered have an annual per capita income level close to $250. These include Honduras ($209), Ecuador ($199), Peru ($241), Algeria ($207), Tunisia ($171), Ivory Coast ($203), Liberia ($154, Rhodesia ($217), Saudi Arabia ($288), Iran ($235), Jordan ($235), and Syria ($203). Just as most countries have some of the very poor, one would expect to find a segment of the population in low income countries with per capita incomes of $250.

Again we are assuming that the recipient country finances part of a development project or program with food aid. To compare with the previous analysis where labor was supplied by low income consumers, we will consider a project that uses 70% labor, 20% domestic goods and services, and 10% imports. On the basis of the earlier studies cited, the medium income consumers are estimated to have an income elasticity of demand for food of approximately 0.73. The Stevens study provides a median value for propensity to consume food of 0.465 at $250, implying a marginal propensity of 0.34.[27]

Seventy units of investment paid as wages to consumers with a marginal propensity to save of 0.09, a marginal taxation rate of 0.09, a marginal propensity to consume imports of 0.08, and a marginal propensity to consume food of 0.34 would generate 17.6 units of demand for retail food. As Ezekiel pointed out, increases in the income level and associated food expenditure result in a larger portion of the food budget being spent on services.[28] If the marketing costs are increased to 20%, the derived demand for wholesale food will be reduced to 14.1 units. The balance of the 51.8 units of disposable income—37.7 units—will be spent on domestic goods and services.

TABLE 1.12.   Aggregate Impact of 100 Units of Investment on Selected Economic Variables in Medium Income Countries

Round	Gross Domestic Income	Savings	Taxes	Imports	Disposable Income	Derived Demand		
						Retail food	Wholesale food	Goods and services
1 (wages)[a]	70.00	6.30	6.30	5.60	51.80	17.61	14.09	37.71
(other)[b]	20.00	1.80	1.80	1.60	14.80	5.03	4.03	10.77
2	48.48	4.36	4.36	3.88	35.88	12.20	9.76	26.12
3	26.12	2.35	2.35	2.09	19.33	6.57	5.26	14.07
4	14.07	1.27	1.27	1.13	10.41	3.54	2.83	7.58
5	7.58	.68	.68	.61	5.61	1.91	1.53	4.08
6	4.08	.37	.37	.33	3.02	1.03	.82	2.20
7	2.20	.20	.20	.18	1.63	.55	.44	1.19
8	1.19	.11	.11	.10	.88	.30	.24	.64
9	.64	.06	.06	.05	.47	.16	.13	.34
10	.34	.03	.03	.03	.25	.08	.07	.18
Total	194.70	17.53	17.53	15.60	144.08	48.98	39.20	104.88

Statistics: Savings = 9%, taxes = 9%, imports = 8%, marginal propensity to consume food = .34, marketing costs = 20%.
a. First-round impact of project expenditures directly for wages.
b. First-round impact of project expenditures for domestic goods and services.

The additional 20 units of the investment used to purchase local equipment, supplies, and services will generate another 4.0 units of demand for wholesale food and 18.0 units of demand for domestic goods and services. Under the assumed parameter estimates for the medium income consumers, first-round impact of 100 units of investment would generate a demand for only 18.1 units of food. Tracing the 48.5 units of income for domestic procedures through the second round adds 9.8 units of food demand. At the end of one year (three rounds) the multiplier effect would generate 164.6 units of domestic income and 33.1 units of food demand. At the end of two years, the derived income is up to 190.3 units and additional food demand to 38.3 units. After ten rounds the total income generated is 194.7 units, of which 39.2 is converted to food demand. Therefore, 84.5% of the total impact is generated in the first year and about 97.0% is generated before the end of the second year (Table 1.12).

If the savings from the first year are assumed to be reinvested in the second year and subject to the multiplier of about 1.64 ($100 invested in the first round generated 164.6 units of income by the end of the third round), the 14.8 units of savings would generate another 24 units of income and 4.8 units of demand for food. Taking expenditure for wages, local supplies, and investment of savings all into account, we estimate that about 43% of development investments in the medium income countries could be financed with food aid without affecting domestic food prices, compared to 57–58% in the low income countries.

In addition to the decline in the amount of derived food demand, derived demand for imports more than doubled from the low income to the medium income case. In the latter case we estimate that 100 units of investment will generate 15.0–15.6 units of import demand, which is a little over 35% of derived food demand. Adding the 10 units of imports needed for the original investment, demand for imports reaches 25.6 units. With a broad definition of commodity aid that includes food and nonfood commodities, the total contract could be raised to 69.6 units (44 units of food and 25.6 units of nonfood) or 69.6% of the original investment. In total, demand for commodity assistance has decreased from the low income case and the composition shifts from about 72% food and 28% nonfood to 63% food and 37% nonfood. An assistance package for the medium income countries that would maximize the use of commodity aid is therefore estimated to include 44.0% food, 25.6% nonfood, and 30.4% capital.

Focusing on a specific country, Tunisia contracted for $16.1 million of commodity aid in 1968 under Title I of P.L. 480. Since $2.4 million of the contract was for cotton and tobacco which were not included as food items when determining consumer demand for food, only $13.7 million of the Tunisia contract represents additional food for which a balancing demand must be generated. Assuming that statistics for the medium income group are rough approximations for Tunisia, $13.7 million of food aid would require about $18.2 million of capital or nonfood commodity for a total investment of $31.9 million if sufficient demand is to be generated to balance the supply of surplus food. An investment of $31.9 million would generate consumer demand for imports amounting to $4.8 million plus the $3.2 million (10% of investment for direct imports to support the investment) for a total of $8.0 million. Assuming that the $2.4 million of cotton and tobacco represented consumer import demand, the balance requiring foreign exchange or nonfood commodity assistance is $5.6 million.

Applying the sixth-round multiplier of 1.9 to the $31.9 million investment, approximately $60.5 million of additional income would be generated in Tunisia over a two-year period. With a national income of 444.0 million dinars or $855 million in 1968 (Official exchange rate was 0.52 dinars per dollar in 1968), an additional $30.25 million of income per year (half of the two-year increase) represents an annual increase of about 3.5%. The minimum increase in employment derived from the investment would be 130,000 man-years if the 70% paid directly for wages on the project represented total payment for labor at the current per capita level ($171 per year). However, a significant portion of income spent on goods and services also represents payment to labor. The maximum employment increase would be achieved if all the $33.2 million income spent on goods and services were paid to labor with no return to other factors of production. Consequently the upper bound on annual employment resulting from the sale of goods and services would be 195,000 man-years at an annual wage rate of $171. The amount of employment generated by the investment is estimated between 130,000 and 325,000 man-years, depending on the proportional return to labor and other resources marketed as goods and services.

HIGH INCOME RECIPIENTS. The third group of countries considered have annual per capita income levels around $450. This group includes Mexico ($478), Costa Rica ($359), Panama ($477), Argentina ($519), Chile ($465), Uruguay ($526), and Barbados ($410).

With stratification of income occurring within countries, many of the other countries would be expected to have segments of the population with incomes at this level.

For consistency with the two previous sections, we will analyze an investment that requires 70% labor, 20% local goods and services, and 10% imports. On the basis of the consumption studies cited, the high income consumers are estimated to have an income elasticity of demand for food of 0.66. Using 0.39 as an estimate of average propensity to consume, a marginal propensity to consume food of 0.26 is implied. Deducting the 26% for savings, taxes, and imports leaves 51.8 units of 70 units paid for wages available to purchase consumer goods. With a marginal propensity to consume food of 0.26, 13.47 units will be spent on food. Raising the marketing cost to 25% to reflect additional services, the net demand for wholesale food would be 10.1 units. Similarly the 20 units used to purchase domestic goods and services would generate 2.89 units of demand for wholesale food. Traced through ten rounds of spending, we estimate that the 100 units of investment will generate 221 units of income and almost 32 units of demand for food.

In contrast to the lower income levels, demand for food represents a smaller portion of the budget and consequently a slower leak from the economy if food demand is balanced with food aid. The resulting impact spreads the respending process over more rounds so that only 79.5% of the impact is generated in the first year (3 rounds), 16.8% in the second year, and 3.7% in the third year. The combination of low marginal propensity to consume food and the longer period over which the multiplier effect is applicable implies that less food aid will be needed in the high income countries, and it will have to be spread over two or three years to balance the availability of food aid with the derived demand.

Closely related to the demand for food and leakage from the economy is the magnitude of the income multiplier. For the high income case the multiplier is estimated at 2.2 over ten rounds compared with 1.49 and 1.95 in the low and medium income cases. At the same time magnitude of derived savings and tax revenue is estimated to rise to about 20% of initial investment compared with the earlier 13.4 and 17.5%. The increase in savings represents a potential for increased private investment and expanded production, and the tax revenue represents a source of increased public investment or revenue to retire the debt for food aid contracts.

At the same time estimates of derived demand for imports increase to 17.7% of the original investment. Adding the 10% for direct

TABLE 1.13. Aggregate Impact of 100 Units of Investment on Selected Economic Variables in High Income Countries

Round	Gross Domestic Income	Savings	Taxes	Imports	Disposable Income	Derived Demand Retail food	Derived Demand Wholesale food	Derived Demand Goods and services
1 (wages)[a]	70.00	6.30	6.30	5.60	51.80	13.47	10.10	41.70
(other)[b]	20.00	1.80	1.80	1.60	14.80	3.85	2.89	11.91
2	53.61	4.82	4.82	4.29	39.67	10.31	7.74	31.94
3	31.94	2.87	2.87	2.56	23.64	6.15	4.61	19.03
4	19.03	1.71	1.71	1.52	14.08	3.66	2.75	11.34
5	11.34	1.02	1.02	.91	8.39	2.18	1.64	6.76
6	6.76	.61	.61	.54	5.00	1.30	.98	4.03
7	4.03	.36	.36	.32	2.98	.77	.58	2.40
8	2.40	.22	.22	.19	1.78	.46	.35	1.43
9	1.43	.13	.13	.11	1.06	.28	.21	.85
10	.85	.08	.08	.07	.63	.16	.12	.51
Total	221.39	19.92	19.92	17.71	163.83	42.59	31.97	131.90

Statistics: Savings = 9%, taxes = 9%, imports = 8%, marginal propensity to consumer food = 0.26, marketing costs = 25%.
a. First-round impact of project expenditures directly for wages.
b. First-round impact of project expenditures for domestic goods and services.

support of the investment pushes the derived demand for imports well over a quarter of the value of the investment plan. Unless significant steps can be taken to develop import substitutes or export earnings, a country experiencing a shortage of foreign exchange will find the balance-of-trade problem critical.

Derived food demand is estimated to reach 25.3% of the investment in one year, 30.7% by the end of two years, and 32.0% at the end of three years. Assuming that the savings from the first round are reinvested in the second round, the 14.8 units would generate 26.0 units of income and 3.7 units of food demand using the first-year income multiplier of 1.76. In the third round the investment from first-round savings is estimated to generate another 5.4 units of income and 0.8 units of demand for food. Total derived food demand for the high income group is estimated to be 36.5 units or 36.5% of the original investment over 3 years with the distribution by year being 25.3, 9.1, and 2.1% respectively (Table 1.13).

For the high income group the aggregate composition of the financing estimated to balance demand with available commodities and to use the maximum amount of commodity aid would be 36.5% food aid, 27.7% nonfood aid equivalent to the import demand, and 35.8% in capital. Presumably the 35.8% above food and import demand could also be provided as commodity aid consisting of goods similar to those produced domestically, but this would reduce the multiplier effect through increased leakage.

Relating to a specific country, Uruguay contracted for $20.6 million of Title I P.L. 480 assistance in 1968: $18.0 million of food and $2.6 million of nonfood commodities. In order to use the $18.0 million dollars of food for development investments without releasing the food aid on the local market system, a total investment of $49.3 million was necessary on the basis of the derived demand estimated previously.

A total investment of $49.3 million (assuming statistics for Uruguay are approximately equal to those estimated for the high income group) would generate approximately $109 million additional income. Given a national income of 141.13 billion pesos in 1967 or $705.65 million (official exchange rate was 200 pesos per dollar), an increase of $109 million over three years represents an annual increase of about 5.1%. If 70% of the initial investment was for labor at a wage rate equal to the present annual per capita income level, employment is estimated to rise by 65,700 man-years. Depending on the labor portion of goods and services, a maximum increase in employment derived indirectly could reach 329,000 man-years (based on 131.9 units of demand for goods and services from the initial investment plus 26.9 additional units from reinvested savings and a per capita income of $526), so the range on derived employment is estimated at 65,700–394,700 man-years over a three-year period. The development investments are estimated to generate $9.9 million of government revenue. In contrast to the low income case where government revenue reached only about 23% of the value of the food aid, revenue in the high income case is estimated to reach approximately 55% of the food contract. This fact alone does not suggest that the return on the food contract to high income countries would be expected to be two and a half times as high as on contracts with low income countries. It must be kept in mind that the $9.9 million of government revenue must service an additional 63.5% of the investment compared with only an additional 42.4% in the low income case.

Demand for imports as a consequence of the investment would equal $13.65 million. Assuming that the $2.6 million of nonfood commodity aid contracted under P.L. 480 would satisfy a similar amount of import demand, a balance of $11.05 million of foreign exchange or nonfood commodity assistance would be needed. Since Uruguay experienced a $22.2 million trade surplus in 1968, commercial imports could be used to satisfy the additional demand for imports.

Using the empirical estimates for low ($75), medium ($250), and high ($450) income countries, derived demand for food was calculated at 57.6% of the initial investment at the low income level, 44.0% at the medium income level, and 36.5% at the high income level (Table 1.14). While the variation in maximum proportion of usable food aid exceeds 20%, the difference under a broader definition of commodity aid is smaller. If nonfood items for which an import demand is derived are included in the commodity aid package, derived demand resulting from investments reaches 79.5% in the low income case and 64.2% in the high income case. For the labor-intensive projects analyzed, the foreign assistance that would most nearly match resource supply and demand while making maximum use of commodity aid would include 60% food, 20% nonfood commodities, and 20% supporting capital for the low income countries; 45% food, 25% nonfood commodities, and 30% supporting capital for medium income countries; and 35% food, 30% nonfood commodities, and 35% supporting capital for high income countries.

FUTURE USEFULNESS OF FOOD AID. The role of food aid in economic development in coming years will depend on the answer to some critical issues that have reduced the efficiency of food aid as a tool for economic development: (1) negative price and produc-

TABLE 1.14. Composition of Foreign Assistance to Maximize Use of Commodity Aid in Development Investments (percent)

Income Group	Food Aid	Nonfood Imports	Supporting Capital
Low	57.6	21.9	20.5
Medium	44.0	25.6	30.4
High	36.5	27.7	35.8

tion impact on domestic producers in recipient countries, (2) hardening of the terms of food aid and lowering of aid component in the shipments, and (3) solution of problems associated with the excess accumulation and utilization of counterpart funds out of past aid agreements. This book is designed primarily to examine these issues empirically and to provide some policy guidelines for both developed and developing countries to enhance the efficiency of food aid as a tool for economic development.

CHAPTER TWO

Price Disincentive Effect in Recipient Countries

F O O D   A I D financed under P.L. 480 has helped to bridge the food gap in recipient countries in early developmental stages and helped meet expanded consumer demand. Serious questions have been raised, however, about potential negative impacts of food aid on recipient countries. Schultz expressed apprehension about price disincentive effects of food aid on agricultural production in recipient countries.[1] Others disagreed with him by either (1) denial of production responsiveness to price changes in developing countries, which rule out any disincentive effect, or (2) acceptance of production responsiveness but disagreement on the degree of such response.[2] The debate on this aspect remained confined to academicians, and larger and larger quantities of food aid kept flowing into the less developed countries (LDCs) to meet the serious shortages of food arising out of the existing development programs. Schultz summed up the situation of agriculture in LDCs: "There is at best little opportunity for growth from traditional agriculture because farmers have exhausted the profitable production possibilities of the state of the arts at their disposal. Better resource allocation and more savings and investment restricted to the factors of production they are employing will not do much for growth."[3] Under these circumstances planners and policy makers were concerned more about keeping rapid increases in food prices in check than about the disincentive effects of food imports on farmers.

Schultz also argued: "Economic growth from the agricultural sector of a poor country depends predominantly upon the availability and price of modern (nontraditional) agricultural factors. The suppliers of these factors in a very real sense hold the key to such growth."[4] These nontraditional factors of production have now become available to agriculturists in most poor countries. In the last few years agricultural programs in LDCs have brought a perceptible technological transformation of agriculture—the so-called Green Revolution—which has rapidly increased output and total net revenue of the agricultural sector.[5] These increases in output have brought food supply into equilibrium with the economic demand (worked out on the basis of per capita incomes and population growth) in some of the food aid recipient countries. Since

37

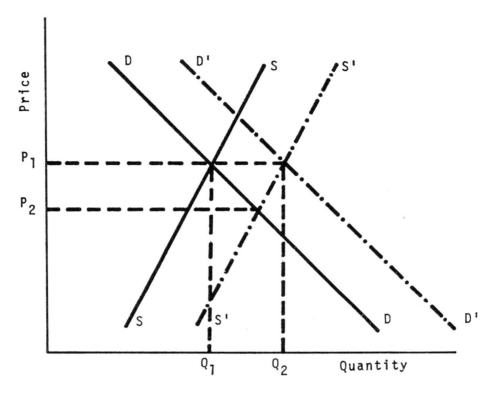

Aggregate food supply and demand equilibrium

Fig. 2.1. Aggregate food supply and demand equilibrium.

a magnitude of unsatisfied nutritional demand still exists, food aid, if available on suitable terms, could be absorbed by creating additional development programs in these countries. (Nutritional demands are worked out on the basis of recommended minimum nutritional requirements of calories and proteins.) But the question of price disincentive effect is more important today than ever before, because the farmers in LDCs are in the process of adopting nontraditional inputs whose expanded use depends on the relative profitability.[6] This leads to a fundamental question of whether food aid necessarily causes price disincentive to farmers in recipient countries or can be absorbed by any means without the disincentive effect. The answer depends on whether the aggregate demand curve can be shifted to move the system to a higher equilibrium point wthout any depression in prices. In Figure 2.1, for example, P.L. 480 imports equal to Q_1Q_2 would depress prices from P_1 to P_2 without a demand shift. However, if demand shifts from D to D' due to the income effects of food aid, prices are not depressed.

REVIEW OF OTHER STUDIES. Since wheat has been the most important single commodity under P.L. 480 aid, most of the studies have concentrated on its price behavior relative to other cereal and noncereal prices. (For a detailed review of studies in the area see Appendix A.) Empirical studies have found that wheat prices have been relatively lower than the prices of other agricultural commodities. Most of the studies have failed to establish a causal relationship between P.L. 480 imports and lower wheat prices and have not quantified production and income impacts of P.L. 480 imports in a systematic and analytical way.

Mann, in his pioneering study, developed an econometric model to measure the price and production impacts of P.L. 480 imports on the Indian economy.[7] The study was based on six simultaneous equations: (1) a supply equation, (2) a demand equation, (3) an income-generation equation, (4) a commercial import equation, (5) a withdrawal-from-stocks equation, and (6) a market clearing identity. Although his model confirmed a negative impact of food aid on prices and agricultural production in India, it contained only one demand equation. He implicitly assumed P.L. 480 import demand to be homogeneous with demand for domestic commodities and that P.L. 480 commodities enter the market in the same way as domestically produced commodities. This in effect ignored the role of mode of distribution adopted to distribute aid commodities and its impact on prices and production in the market for domestic producers. The role of the method of distribution in minimizing price and production impact of food aid has been emphasized by Fisher.[8] Fisher argues that Schultz and others have overstated the negative price effects of food aid by implicitly assuming that (1) the elasticity of domestic supply is zero and (2) there is a single market for imported and domestic commodities so distribution of concessional imports substitutes directly for domestic demand.

Markets for domestically produced commodities and for the same commodity supplied through imports are not perfectly homogeneous; hence demand for domestic commodities is not directly substituted by imported food grains, particularly in India, which Schultz used as an illustration. Fisher argues that the negative impact of food aid can be reduced if it is distributed outside the market for domestic production so that distribution creates additional demand. The objective of the analysis that follows is to develop a theoretical model to test Fisher's hypothesis—namely, that the negative effect of food aid on prices and production is much less (or could be absent) under a differentiated market situation. If Fisher's theoretical argument can be supported empirically, previous analytical work that neglected the real income effect on demand promises to have overestimated the negative impact of P.L. 480. We have considered market differentiation under two types of approaches: the program approach and the project approach.

PROGRAM APPROACH. The concept of market differentiation is incorporated in Mann's analytical framework by including an additional equation so the system provides for cereal purchases on the open market and the concessional market at lower prices. Incorporating a second "demand" equation and modifying various other equations in the basic Mann model brings stronger causal relationships and improves their reliability. The model is specified by defining several a priori functional relationships that are presumed to exist as indicated by economic theory.

The data used in the analysis relate to India for 1956–67, but the framework is of wider interest because it can be used to make improved estimates of the impact of aid on recipient countries that do have a differentiated market situation (and followed a program approach) and, more importantly, as a guide for administering food aid to minimize negative price and production effects in recipient countries while maximizing beneficial effects. We use the term *program approach* to represent a case where food aid commodities are not linked with a particular project. In India P.L. 480 supplies were channeled through a system of fair-price shops, which are government-licensed food shops. Channeling the supplies through the fair-price shops rather than releasing them into the open market represented market differentiation. As the system of fair-price shops has functioned it has not been completely isolated from the open market; the food grains are available "at specified and more or less fixed prices and in given quantities to each consumer."[9] Consumers have been free to buy either from a fair-price shop or in the open market or in both. So instead of complete isolation of markets there has been some degree of interdependence. Still the release of inferior quality of wheat (in terms of Indian consumer preference) at artificially low prices mainly to poorer sections, both in surplus as well as deficit states, does justify its treatment as a separate market.

The Model. The model includes a supply equation, an open market demand equation, a concessional market distribution equation (representing demand under fixed price and controlled supply rather than demand), an income equation, a commercial import equation, a withdrawal-from-stocks equation, and an excess demand equation. The reduced form of the system of seven equations provides estimates for the quantitative impact of P.L. 480 shipments of cereals distributed through a concessional market arrangement. Specification of these relationships is explained below.

SUPPLY OF CEREALS IN CURRENT PERIOD. The quantity available for consumption from domestic production in a particular year is primarily the result of production decisions, weather conditions, and available technology before and during the growing season. Supply from the domestic sources in period t is a function of production during the agricultural year $t - 1$ (July 1970–June 1971), and production in turn has been found to be a function of price in the preceding agricultural year (1969–70). In developing countries that lack an effective market forecasting system, the cultivator's primary source of information is prices received for the previous crop. Thus supply becomes a function of prices in period $t - 2$. Rainfall in period $t - 1$ (R_{t-1}) and cereal yield (T_{t-1}), as a proxy for technology, have a direct impact on production. T_{t-1} and R_{t-1} are used to account for the contribution of both factors to production. (Although rainfall and yield would appear to create a problem of multicollinearity, the basic data indicate that the correlation between the two variables is only 0.10.) The theoretical supply function thus is specified as

$$Q_t^s = f_1 \ (P_{t-2}^c, \ R_{t-1}, \ T_{t-1}) \tag{2.1}$$

where

$\quad Q_t^s =$ per capita quantity of cereals available from domestic production for consumption in period t

$P_{t-2}^c =$ deflated index of wholesale prices of cereals in the period before production

$R_{t-1} =$ rainfall index as a proxy for weather conditions during the producing season

$T_{t-1} =$ cereal yield as a proxy for other factors affecting adoption of technology

OPEN MARKET DEMAND FOR CEREALS. Economic theory states that quantity
demanded per capita is a function of the price of the commodity itself, the price of related commodities, and income
level. Thus the open market demand equation is specified as

$$Q_t^d = f_2 \ (P_t^c, \ P_t^r, \ Y_t) \qquad\qquad (2.2)$$

where

$Q_t^d =$ per capita quantity of cereals demanded in the open
market for consumption in period t
$P_t^c =$ index of deflated wholesale prices of cereal in period t
$P_t^r =$ deflated price of noncereal foods in period t
$Y_t =$ deflated per capita consumer income in period t

Strictly speaking, the supply equation is formulated in terms of
wholesale prices and the demand equation in terms of retail prices. But
with an assumption about constant marketing margins, a demand function can be derived in terms of wholesale prices.

DISTRIBUTION FROM CONCESSIONAL MARKET. Distribution of P.L. 480 imports through the concessional market is a function of economic
variables at the minimum level and, because of the fixed price
offering, physical restraint at the upper level. Some consumers consider
imported cereals an inferior commodity and continue to purchase cereals
in the open market even when there is some price differential between
open market and concessional markets. As the two prices diverge, however, more and more consumers are willing to substitute imported cereals
for domestic cereals. Consequently the demand for cereals through the
concessional market is a function of price at the concessional market itself, price of substitute cereals in the open market, and income level of
consumers.

At the upper limit, price adjustment cannot serve as a balancing
mechanism to equate demand with a limited supply, because the price
is fixed by the government and has been held relatively constant. Consequently the upper limit on distribution through the fair-price shops is
the quantity that the government chooses to release for distribution.
Since the primary source of commodities for distribution through the
fair-price shops has been P.L. 480 imports, the quantity of imports is
entered in the concessional distribution equation as a proxy for the

maximum quantity available for distribution.[10] The concessional distribution is specified as

$$Q_t^c = f_3 \ (P_t^p, \ P_t^c, \ Y_t, \ M_t^p \tag{2.3}$$

where

Q_t^c = per capita quantity of cereals distributed through the concessional market in period t

P_t^p = predetermined cereal price charged in the concessional market (deflated by consumer price index) in period t

M_t^p = per capita quantity of concessional imports of cereal under P.L. 480 in period t

INCOME. The economy in developing countries usually is dominated by the agricultural sector. Hence agricultural output constitutes a large portion of national income, and fluctuations in this output have a significant impact on aggregate income. In the Indian economy the industrial sector is second in importance. The third major income source in India is government expenditure, particularly through the involvement of the government in financing development investments. Thus the income equation is specified as

$$Y_t = f_4 \ (Q_t^s, \ Q_t^i, \ G_t) \tag{2.4}$$

where

Q_t^i = value of per capita industrial output (deflated by consumer price index)

G_t = deflated per capita government expenditure in period t

COMMERCIAL IMPORTS. Commercial imports of cereals in India serve as a government policy instrument to relieve inflationary pressure on food prices when and where domestic food shortages occur. In this role the government imports food to satisfy consumer demand, and commercial imports of cereals are effectively a function of the same factors that determine the demand for cereals in the open market. The commercial import equation is specified as

$$M_t^o = f_5 \ (P_t^c, \ P_t^r, \ Y_t) \tag{2.5}$$

where

$M_t^o =$ per capita quantity of commercial import of cereals in period t

WITHDRAWAL FROM GOVERNMENT STOCKS. Withdrawals from government stocks provide a residual source of cereals to balance other government programs. As the government increases internal procurement of domestic cereals to support prices, the need for net withdrawals to control inflation of cereal prices and to satisfy other government demand (such as feeding military personnel and inhabitants of public institutions) decreases. In the opposite direction, as the government increases the availability of cereals for distribution through the concessional market, withdrawals from government stocks must increase if other sources of supply remain constant. Finally, commercial and concessional imports are alternative sources for satisfying government demand for various programs, so withdrawals from government stocks are a function of the level of import activities. The withdrawal equation is defined as

$$W_t = f_6 \; (Q_t^c, \; M_t^o, \; M_t^p, \; C_t^p) \tag{2.6}$$

where

$W_t =$ per capita net withdrawals of cereals from government stocks in period t

$W_t^p =$ per capita internal procurement of cereals by the government in period t

MARKET CLEARING. The last equation, a market identity equation to close the system by forcing excess demand for cereals to be equal to zero, is specified as

$$Q_t^d + Q_t^c - Q_t^s - M_t^p - M_t^o - W_t = 0 \tag{2.7}$$

The model consists of seven equations and 16 variables. Since the purpose of this model is to evaluate the economic impact of P.L. 480 imports on prices and domestic supply of cereals, certain variables are treated as predetermined or given outside the system. The predetermined or exogenous variables include T_{t-1}, R_{t-1}, P_t^r, P_t^p, C_t^p, M_t^p, G_t, P_{t-2}^c, and Q_t^i. The values for these variables are given at a particular time and are not subject to determination by the econometric model. Seven variables—Q_t^s, Q_t^d, Q_t^c, P_t^c, Y_t, M_t^o, and W_t—are classified as endogenous.

Empirical Results. The seven structural equations provide the joint interactions of the variables in the system. To provide for independent examination and analysis of the jointly determined variables, the system is solved to obtain the reduced form in which each endogenous variable is uniquely defined as a function of the exogenous variables and the constraints of the system in the derived reduced form.

Equations (2.2) through (2.6) are overidentified.[11] Under conditions of overidentification, the two-stage least squares methods of regression provides consistent estimates of coefficients of the structural form. With estimates of the coefficients for the endogenous variables (β's) and the predetermined variables (Γ's), the reduced form coefficients can be derived as

$$\pi^* = \beta^{*-1} \Gamma^* \qquad\qquad (2.8)$$

where

$\pi^* =$ the matrix of estimated reduced form coefficients
$\beta^* =$ the matrix of estimated coefficients of endogenous variables
$\Gamma^* =$ the matrix of estimated coefficients of predetermined variables

The structural equations of models have been estimated by using data from the Indian economy during 1956–67 collected from a number of published sources (see Appendix Table C.1). Except for (2.1), two-stage least squares method was used to estimate coefficients for the structural equations. Because (2.1) contains no endogenous variables as independent variables, ordinary least squares were used to estimate the associated coefficients. The estimated coefficients for the structural equations are presented in Table 2.1. The variables are as defined earlier. Signs of nearly all coefficients for the estimated equations agree with economic theory.

The supply equation has positive signs for all three independent variables, indicating that the supply of cereals Q_t^s reacts positively to increases in the weather variables R_{t-1}, the proxy for technology T_{t-1}, and price P_{t-2}^c. The estimated price elasticity of supply at the mean is

TABLE 2.1. Two-Stage Least Squares Estimates of Structural Equations

Equation	Estimated Equation
$(2.1)^a$	$Q_t{}^s = -13.89343 + 0.09118T_{t-1} + 0.56808R_{t-1} + 0.24424P_{t-2}{}^c$ $\quad\quad\quad\quad\quad(0.02665)\quad\quad\quad(0.12615)\quad\quad\quad(0.31964)$
(2.2)	$Q_t{}^d = -10.54661 - 0.553321P_t{}^c + 0.72847Y_t + 0.047698P_t{}^r$ $\quad\quad\quad\quad\quad\quad(0.34411)\quad\quad\quad(0.14954)\quad\quad\quad(0.28149)$
(2.3)	$Q_t{}^c = 60.91986 + 0.209881P_t{}^c - 0.251656Y_t - 0.22217P_t{}^p + 0.89376M_t{}^p$ $\quad\quad\quad\quad\quad\quad(0.23572)\quad\quad\quad(0.09075)\quad\quad\quad(0.14373)\quad\quad\quad(0.389855)$
(2.4)	$Y_t = 118.91530 + 0.80042Q_t{}^s + 0.28386Q_t{}^i - 0.00092G_t$ $\quad\quad\quad\quad\quad\quad(0.39448)\quad\quad\quad(0.25924)\quad\quad\quad(0.00089)$
(2.5)	$M_t{}^o = 27.84666 + 0.09045P_t{}^c - 0.14608Y_t + 0.03172P_t{}^r$ $\quad\quad\quad\quad\quad\quad(0.10881)\quad\quad\quad(0.04729)\quad\quad\quad(0.08901)$
(2.6)	$W_t = 1.52758 + 0.97393Q_t{}^c - 0.53602M_t{}^o - 1.62118C_t{}^p - 0.89938M_t{}^p$ $\quad\quad\quad\quad\quad(0.17889)\quad\quad\quad(0.39028)\quad\quad\quad(0.47693)\quad\quad\quad(0.22458)$

Note: Asymptotic standard errors are given in parentheses below the estimated coefficients.

a. Coefficients estimated by ordinary least squares.

0.156, which compares with National Council of Applied Economic Research estimates of 0.22 for rice, 0.16 for wheat, and 0.16 for barley.[12]

The open market demand equation has signs on all coefficients that agree with economic theory, indicating that demand for cereals $Q_t{}^d$ is positively correlated with price of other food $P_t{}^r$ and changes in income Y_t. (We considered an alternative formulation of the open market demand equation which included the price charged at the fair-price shops, but the regression coefficient was insignificant even at low levels, so the concessional price was excluded from the final equation.) The estimated price elasticity of demand is -0.39, slightly higher than the National Councils' estimate of -0.34.

The concessional market distribution equation indicates that $Q_t{}^c$ is positively correlated with the price of cereals in the open market $P_t{}^c$ and negatively correlated with income level Y_t and the price of cereals at the fair-price shops $P_t{}^p$. (An alternative formulation of the concessional distribution equation included price of other food, but the regression coefficient was insignificant even at low levels and caused the ratio of regression sum of squares to residual sum of squares to decrease.) The relatively large coefficient on $M_t{}^p$ supports the argument that distribution through the concessional market is highly correlated with imports under P.L. 480 and associated decisions to make these commodities available for distribution through the fair-price shops.

The income equation indicates that an increase in Y_t is positively correlated with agricultural supply $Q_t{}^s$ and industrial supply $Q_t{}^i$ but negatively correlated with government expenditure G_t. The sign on government expenditure is not in conformity with the logic of economic

TABLE 2.2. Correlation Coefficients for Government Expenditure and Income

	Government Expenditure	Deflated Government Expenditure
Aggregate income	0.9625	0.7633
Per capita income	0.9515	0.7483
Deflated per capita income	−0.5568	−0.2228

theory. In examining the correlation matrix for the variables in the equation (Table 2.2), it was noted that government expenditure has been positively correlated with both aggregate income and per capita income but negatively correlated with the deflated or real income. If the sign is opposite for per capita income and per capita income divided by price, price level must be increasing faster than per capita income to make real per capita income decline. This decline is interpreted to mean that although government expenditure has caused an increase in money incomes, it has also caused prices to rise enough to force up the consumer price index faster than money income with a negative impact on real income for the period under study.

The commercial import equation indicates that imports vary inversely with per capita income level Y_t and directly with prices of cereals P_t^c and other food P_t^r. (We considered some alternative forms of the impact equation which included concessional imports and the ratio of cereal prices to other food prices, but regression coefficients for both were insignificant even at low levels.) This variation supports the contention that imported cereals are substitutes for domestic food and not complements. The stock equation indicates that withdrawals W_t are directly related to distribution through the fair-price shops Q_t^c and inversely related to commercial imports M_t^o, internal procurement C_t^p, and P.L. 480 imports M_t^p. (Alternative forms of the withdrawal equation were considered which included consumer demand factors such as prices of cereals and other food and income levels, but none of the regressions of this nature produced ratios of regression to residual sum of squares that exceeded 1.0 and consequently were insignificant.)

The estimated reduced form coefficients of particular interest to this study are those associated with variable M_t^p or P.L. 480 imports (Table 2.3). The coefficients or impact multipliers from the reduced form model indicate that increasing P.L. 480 imports by 1 kg per capita depresses cereal prices by 0.1314 unit (π^*_{47}) of the price index, increases demand by 0.0727 kg per capita (π^*_{27}), and increases concessional distribution by 0.8557 kg per capita (π^*_{37}). Consequently 92.84% of the increase

TABLE 2.3. Estimated Reduced Form Coefficients to Measure Impact of P.L. 480 Imports on the Indian Economy, 1956–67

	Intercept	T_{t-1}	R_{t-1}	P_t^r	P_t^p	C_t^p	M_t^p	G_t	P_{t-2}^c	Q_t^i
Q_t^s	−13.8934	0.0912	0.5681	0.0	0.0	0.0	0.0	0.0	0.2442	0.0
Q_t^d	−5.9505	0.0847	0.5275	0.0168	0.0054	−1.5250	0.0727	0.0	0.2268	−0.0043
Q_t^c	7.2528	−0.0349	−0.2173	0.0162	−0.2250	0.7989	0.8557	−0.0001	−0.0934	0.0391
P_t^c	133.6264	−0.0569	−0.3547	0.5578	−0.0098	2.7561	−0.1314	−0.0012	−0.1525	0.3815
Y_t	107.7947	0.0730	0.4547	0.0	0.0	0.2493	0.0	−0.0009	0.1955	0.2839
M_t^o	24.1866	−0.0158	−0.0985	−0.0368	−0.0009	0.2493	−0.0119	0.0	−0.0424	−0.0070
W_t	56.2758	−0.0256	−0.1593	−0.0038	−0.2189	−0.9754	−0.0597	−0.0001	−0.0685	0.0418

in P.L. 480 imports would result in increased consumption. As an example, data indicate that P.L. 480 imports for 1967 (4.055 million metric tons) increased consumption by 3.771 million metric tons or about 7.38 kg per capita for the year. Associated with a 1 kg per capita increase in P.L. 480 imports was a 0.0119 kg (π^*_{67}) decrease in commercial imports and a 0.0597 kg (π^*_{77}) withdrawal from government stocks. Due to the time lag in supply response, supply is unaffected in period t.

To measure the price impact in succeeding years, it is necessary to use a delay multiplier that equals $\pi^*_{47} \pi^*_{49}{}^{\frac{1}{2}P}$, where $P = 0, 2, 4, 6, \ldots$, because of a two-year lag between $P_t{}^c$ and $P_{t-2}{}^c$. Therefore, the delay multiplier for cereal price is 0.003056 in the fourth year, and 0.000466 in the sixth year. The first delay multiplier represents a change of less than 0.03%, using the mean values of the price index and the multiplier values of the price index and the multiplier values in the succeeding years as essentially zero.

The impact on supply (Table 2.4) is measured by the delay multiplier $\pi^*_{19} \pi^*_{47} \pi^*_{49}{}^{\frac{1}{2}P-1}$, where $P = 2, 4, 6, \ldots$, because of the time lag of price impact on production. Evaluated at $P = 2$ to measure the impact of a change in price during the period when P.L. 480 imports occur on production two years later, the delay multiplier is -0.032088. In India each ton per capita of cereals supplied through P.L. 480 depresses the domestic supply by 0.032088 ton per capita during the production season two years later. Similarly, at $P = 4$ the multiplier is 0.004893, so the impact of one ton of P.L. 480 cereals results in 0.004893 ton per capita of increased cereal production. At $P = 6$ the multiplier is again negative at -0.000746. In quantity terms at the mean population of India in 1956–67, P.L. 480 imports of 1 kg per capita (450,480 metric tons) of cereals are estimated to have depressed domestic production by 14.445 metric tons two years later, increased production by 2,204 metric tons

TABLE 2.4. Total Effect of P.L. 480 Imports on Domestic Production in India

Year	Delay Multipliers	Cumulated Multipliers
2	—0.032088	—0.032088
4	0.004893	—0.027195
6	—0.000746	—0.027941
8	0.000114	—0.027827
10	—0.000017	—0.027844
12	0.000003	—0.027841
14	. . .	—0.027841

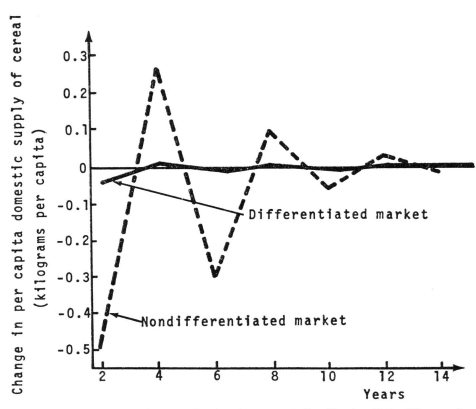

*Fig. 2.2. Multiperiod production impact of distributing P.L. 480 cereal
(one kilogram per capita) under alternative market conditions.*

four years later, and depressed production by 336 metric tons six years
later.

The net impact on supply is most accurately measured by the cumulated multipliers over several years. Each kilogram of P.L. 480 cereals
is estimated to have depressed production of cereals by 0.027841 kg, so for
each 450,480 metric tons of imports, production was depressed by 12,600
tons over a 14-year period, with the major impact coming as a result of
the first and second round of price changes. Comparing our estimates of
multipliers with Mann's (Fig. 2.2), the cumulative impact of distribution
through a differentiated market is about one-tenth the impact with a
nondifferentiated market.

Thus the above model differs uniquely from previous attempts
to evaluate the impact of P.L. 480 imports on recipient economies. It ex-

plicitly incorporates variables to account for the case where P.L. 480 imports are distributed to consumers in a manner that creates a shift in demand as well as a shift in total supply. For a price elasticity of demand of —0.39 a decrease in price of 0.1314 implies a change in quantity demanded of 0.07227 kg per capita if adjustments were made along the demand curve, compared to the actual increase of 0.9284 kg per capita implying a shift in demand. With the shift in demand as well as supply allowed, the impact of P.L. 480 imports on domestic supply is estimated to be less than 9% of the magnitude estimated by Mann, who assumed only a shift in supply. In contrast to a reduction in domestic supply of 143,200 metric tons as estimated by Mann, the revised cumulated multiplier we derived implies a negative impact of only 12,600 metric tons on domestic supply over a 14-year period.

For policy formulation and application, the conclusion of this analysis indicates that the negative impact of P.L. 480 imports on domestic prices and supply can be significantly reduced if the commodities are distributed in the recipient economy in a way that creates new demand rather than substituting for or competing with the existing demand. The analysis indicates that distribution through fair-price shops in India has provided for increased consumption amounting to 93% of the amount of commodities imported. Since fair-price shop distribution is at a lower price than the open market price, distribution through these shops has increased consumer welfare by increasing consumption and lowering prices. At the same time the distribution of P.L. 480 commodities has depressed domestic prices in the open market by only 0.02%. Thus the analysis supports Fisher's theoretical hypothesis that distribution under a differentiated market situation will minimize price and production impacts of food aid and implies that previous studies have underestimated the net contribution of food aid to domestic supply because the income effect of distributing food aid at concessional prices has been ignored.

Interregional Availability. The model developed above does not reveal one more important contribution of P.L. 480 aid in improving the interregional distribution of per capita availability. Again we illustrate this aspect of P.L. 480 aid by analyzing the situation in India. The shortage of calorie availability probably is more acute for lower income groups than at the national level, because calorie consumption of economically well-off sections of the population is generally considered much higher than the recommended minimum.[13] The nutritional levels of these vulnerable sections must be lower than the all-India average. A similar argument applies to the various states and regions

TABLE 2.5. Per Capita Availability of Cereals (including imports) during 1957–68 (kg/year)

Years	Andhra Pradesh	Assam	Bihar	Gujrat	Kerala	Madhya Pradesh	Maharastra	Mysore	Orissa	Punjab & Hariyana	Rajasthan	Tamil Nadu	Uttar Pradesh	West Bengal	Coefficient of Variation
1957	120.8	139.9	100.5	61.9	60.8	184.6	137.2	117.4	150.2	159.4	149.7	120.9	115.8	129.4	27.42
1958	126.6	133.0	89.3	77.2	62.0	153.7	129.8	127.5	157.6	163.4	147.0	122.1	113.2	127.9	24.74
1959	144.1	132.2	118.5	108.4	65.4	194.2	148.5	134.5	164.5	196.8	159.4	122.4	121.0	132.6	22.77
1960	144.4	132.5	117.9	105.4	64.8	184.9	146.9	140.8	171.1	160.6	160.4	132.2	122.7	149.4	21.70
1961	149.4	137.1	126.5	81.1	69.6	211.9	163.9	135.7	189.9	206.9	145.4	141.2	131.6	154.6	26.42
1962	176.0	137.8	122.4	106.0	65.1	197.5	138.3	138.7	187.7	200.5	174.9	150.6	133.0	139.7	24.37
1963	139.5	125.9	119.6	93.3	65.5	179.1	133.7	139.3	184.6	184.9	159.0	144.2	121.4	140.7	23.28
1964	151.4	139.8	125.0	118.9	81.5	194.5	149.1	144.0	207.1	201.1	146.9	148.1	117.7	149.9	15.22
1965	145.7	136.8	123.1	136.9	118.7	193.5	151.0	150.7	196.5	195.7	162.7	142.5	130.8	157.6	16.27
1966	132.4	138.6	112.4	109.9	103.9	139.2	120.7	116.5	152.1	174.3	138.1	134.5	113.2	150.8	14.25
1967	155.6	116.4	91.6	106.5	102.8	131.1	126.4	131.3	169.6	160.2	143.7	134.6	112.7	133.2	16.58
1968	141.5	134.0	127.9	126.9	98.8	185.6	139.0	144.3	172.3	185.8	175.2	143.6	132.4	147.8	16.14
Coefficient of Variation (%)	10.57	18.64	13.66	20.56	25.65	13.17	9.15	7.74	10.31	9.91	7.74	7.58	6.53	7.17	

Source: Directorate of Economics and Statistics, *Bulletin of Food Statistics* (New Delhi: GOI, 1956 to 1970).

within this vast subcontinent. Punjab and Rajasthan have a surplus of wheat; Bihar, Uttar Pradesh, and Madhya Pradesh are deficient. Similarly Andhra Pradesh, Madhya Pradesh, Orissa, and Madras have surplus rice; Bihar, Maharastra, West Bengal, and Kerala have a deficit.

Normally we would expect that, given free movement of food grains from one place to another, the differences in per capita supply between states would be a function of the rate of growth of income and population. But in the atmosphere of general scarcity free trade does not perform this equalizing function. From 1959 on, restrictions on intrazonal movement of food grains from one state to another or on interzonal transfer where each zone comprises a number of states have been operative. The idea behind such zones was to procure the excess food grains from the surplus states and distribute them in the deficit states, but the requirements from the public distribution system (fair-price shops) have increased much faster than procurement. Consequently P.L. 480 imports became the main plank of the government distribution of cereals through the system of the fair-price shops, and the role of P.L. 480 imports in improving the distribution of cereals over the years between states becomes important. We have computed the coefficient of variation for per capita net availability between states and also over the years within the same states (Table 2.5).

We worked out the per capita net availability of cereals by accounting for their procurement, movement across the states, and distribution. These figures include distribution from imported supplies. Availabilities show considerable variation. The states of Kerala, Gujrat, Assam, Bihar, and Madhya Pradesh show a much higher variation than the other states. The coefficient of variation of intrastate availability from year to year has been fairly high. However, we noted that the coefficient dropped from 27.42 in 1957 to 16.14 in 1968. We also found that the public distribution of food grains went up during this period. Supplies for the public distribution were derived from P.L. 480 imports and other sources which include non-P.L. 480 imports, domestic procurement, and withdrawals from stocks. To work out the effect of P.L. 480 and non-P.L. 480 components of public distribution on the coefficient of variation, we have fitted the following regression equation to the data from 1957 to 1968:

$$C_v = 29.635 - 1.3671 M_t^p - 0.9330 O_t \qquad R^2 = 0.99$$
$$\quad\quad\quad\quad (3.534) \quad\quad (3.691) \qquad\qquad\qquad (2.9)$$

where

C_v = coefficient of variation of net per capita availability of cereals among the states

M_t^p = P.L. 480 supplies of cereals in million tons

O_t = supplies from other sources in million tons. Other sources include non-P.L. 480 imports, domestic procurement, plus or minus changes in stocks

The numbers in parentheses are "t" values for estimated coefficients.

This equation shows that the effect of P.L. 480 supplies on the statewise coefficient of variation in cereal availability has been highly significant. If nothing had been done through the release of supplies from the fair-price shops, the coefficient of variation would have been 29.64. An additional 1 million tons of cereals under P.L. 480 has brought down the coefficient of variation by 1.37; the increase of 1 million tons of non-P.L. 480 supplies has brought down the coefficient of variation by 0.99. Thus the release of P.L. 480 food aid through the fair-price shops has improved the interregional distribution of cereals in India.

PROJECT APPROACH. Food aid commodities were absorbed in the general development program in India Unlike India, many recipient countries have used food aid for raising additional development projects, and food aid supplies have been linked with these projects. Under the project approach, price, production, and income impacts of aid must be evaluated in a different framework. A differentiated market can still be created by releasing the aid supplies to restricted groups of recipients at market prices (or at lower than market prices). We have developed a simplified partial equilibrium model to evaluate the impact of P.L. 480 under the project approach.

The Model. In the model, demand is specified as a function of P and a coefficient b represents the impact of all other variables on demand; e is the price elasticity of demand.

$$Q_d = bP^e \tag{2.10}$$

Similarly, supply is specified as a function of price and a coefficient c representing the impact of all other variables on supply; ϵ is the price elasticity of supply.

$$Q_s = cP^\epsilon \tag{2.11}$$

The equilibrium price equating supply and demand is reached by setting the supply and demand equations equal and solving for price. To simplify the manipulation of subsequent equations, $-\xi$ is defined to equal $(e - \epsilon)^{-1}$.

$$P_1 = b^\xi c^{-\xi} \tag{2.12}$$

Substituting (2.12) into either (2.10) or (2.11) provides the equilibrium quantity where supply

$$Q_d = b^{1+\xi e} c^{-\xi e} \tag{2.13a}$$

or

$$Q_s = b^{\xi\epsilon} c^{1-\xi\epsilon} \tag{2.13b}$$

and demand are equal. The impact of a shift in supply and/or demand on the equilibrium price and quantity is reached by multiplying (2.10) and (2.11) by shift factors and recalculating price and quantity.[14] Using Γ as the shift factor for demand and Ψ as the shift factor for supply, the new equilibrium price is

$$P_2 = (\Gamma b)^\xi (\Psi c)^{-\xi} \tag{2.14}$$

so the relationship between new and old price is

$$P_2 = (\Gamma^\xi \Psi^{-\xi}) P_1 \tag{2.15}$$

The new equilibrium quantity is

$$Q_2 = (b\Gamma)^{1+\xi e}(c\Psi)^{-\xi e} \tag{2.16a}$$

or

$$Q_2 = (b\Gamma)^{\xi\epsilon}(c\Psi)^{1-\xi\epsilon} \tag{2.16b}$$

and the relationship between the new and old quantity is

$$Q_2 = (\Gamma^{1+\xi\epsilon}\Psi^{-\xi\epsilon}) Q_1 \tag{2.17a}$$

or

$$Q_2 = (\Gamma^{\xi\epsilon}\Psi^{1-\xi\epsilon})\, Q_1 \tag{2.17b}$$

To illustrate the working of the above model, we take the case where food is given as a grant. Let us assume that food aid grants amounting to 5% of the domestic supply at the previous equilibrium are provided to a group of low income consumers with marginal propensity to consume food at or near 1.0. With the magnitude of the horizontal shift in supply equal to 5%, Ψ takes a value of 1.05. Assuming that the P.L. 480 commodities have a market value equal to the domestic commodities,[15] the horizontal shift in the demand curve Γ resulting from a change in income is equal to 1.0 plus the marginal propensity to consume food times ($\Psi - 1.0$). With marginal propensity to consume (MPC) equal to or near 1.0 for this group,

$$\Gamma = 1.0 + (MPC_{food})\, \Psi \tag{2.18}$$

food grants would increase demand by an amount equal to the additional supply, and Γ would also be of the magnitude of 1.05. When Γ is equal to Ψ there is no change in price, because the new supply and demand are just equal at the old price.

Consequently, with very low income consumers receiving food grants, impact of food aid on the economy would be negligible. The additional food supply in the market system has little effect because the income effect of the grants motivates consumers to increase their demand by a similar amount. As a result of an equal shift in supply and demand, there would be no price effect to stimulate additional demand for domestic food and no price effect to disrupt domestic supply. With the strong preference for food, grant recipients would not trade away any significant amount of food for nonfood items, so there would be no effect on demand for output from the industrial sector. With no change in prices or domestic supply, there would be no effect on income in either the agricultural or industrial sector aside from the increase in income realized by the grant recipients.

From a welfare standpoint, the grants would have an immediate impact by increasing food consumption for the recipients but no lasting positive impact after the grants were discontinued. Upon termination of the grants, total supply would shift back to the domestic and commercial import level. At the same time the loss of income in the form of food grants would shift the effective demand back to the levels existing before the availability of the grants. The only lasting effect of the grants would be the investment in human capital. In actual practice, however, the recipient countries are interested in more tangible development projects, and marginal propensity of income recipients to consume is less than unity. Therefore, we have considered price, production, and income impacts of work-type projects in the framework of above model.

Work Projects. Unlike distribution of food aid through grant programs, distribution through work projects implies a more restricted group of recipients. Work projects basically limit recipients to the same individuals who would be available to earn regular wages if such employment opportunities existed. Although it is possible for work projects to be competitive with other job opportunities, there would be no competition unless wage-in-kind rates were set above competitive wage rates. The shift of previously employed workers to work projects would be inefficient because of the transitional unemployment it would create and the effect of locating "permanent" employees in "temporary" employment provided by work projects. Establishing wage-in-kind rates below competitive wage rates would offer a greater attraction for unemployed and underemployed workers to take advantage of the opportunities available through the work projects than for those who are employed.

Wage-in-kind payments have essentially the same impact on consumption patterns and domestic production that grants do, with one major exception. In both cases distribution of food aid commodities represents a shift in the aggregate food supply of the recipient country and a shift in demand that depends on the marginal preference to consume food from incremental income. The intersection of the two new schedules determines the new price and quantity relationship that will exist after the shift. The difference occurs in the additional shift in the supply curve directly related to the use of the labor provided for the project.

The amount of permanent or long-run shift in supply to be achieved depends on the nature of work projects financed with food aid. The three broad classes include direct production, short-run overheads, and long-run overheads. The direct production involves use of labor to provide goods and services for immediate consumption. Using food aid to finance direct production would have the greatest impact on short-run supply but the least impact on long-run supply. Short-run investments might include construction of dams and irrigation canals, clearing land for cultivation, building a fertilizer plant, or similar projects of relatively short-run nature that would have a direct effect on production in the immediate future. Long-run overhead investments might include construction of modern transportation systems, building schools, training teachers, construction of improved housing, and similar projects that affect the welfare of the people but have a much longer and indirect impact on productivity of human resources and ultimately the supply of goods and services produced.

The impact on productivity is another function of the allocation of work projects between the agricultural sector and the industrial sector. It is possible to allocate a major portion to the agricultural sector so agricultural production would be directly affected. On the other hand, all the work projects might be allocated to the industrial sector so that agricultural output was unaffected. Consequently the impact of P.L. 480 commodities on agricultural supply, when used to finance work projects, depends on the allocation of the projects between sectors, the relation between nutrition and productivity, and the rate at which the projects mature.

To analyze the impact of food aid used as wages-in-kind on work projects under alternative assumptions about productivity, we considered several allocations of investment and rates of return. Generally, unemployed laborers would be expected to respond to opportunities offered by work projects, and they would be characterized by low levels of income.

As in the example where P.L. 480 commodities were distributed as grants, adding food aid to the system would shift the total supply schedule to the right. Use of the food as wages-in-kind increases real income of recipients and also shifts the aggregate demand function to the right. With a marginal propensity to consume food of less than 1.0, the demand curve would shift to the right by some amount less than the supply shift. Since food aid supplied as wages-in-kind is relatively difficult to exchange on the market for other commodities, most of it will be consumed directly by the recipient, with any marginal allocation of income for nonfood commodities coming at the expense of domestic agricultural production. Any decline in demand for domestic agricultural commodities will have a negative impact on prices and ultimately on production. Although a decline in agricultural prices would shift the terms of trade in favor of food for consumers and stimulate an increase in quantity demanded, price elasticities of less than 1.0 exclude the possibilities of maintaining preprogram income levels for agricultural workers.

In the first case a situation is considered where all projects are in agriculture and represent social overhead investment that increases the productivity of all resources proportionately. Examples of work projects used to develop factors of production in agriculture include land clearing and drainage in Colombia, forest development in Japan, and electric power development in Pakistan and Brazil. Development of factor productivity stimulates a shift in domestic supply of agricultural commodities. The shift in supply causes a depression of consumer prices, which in turn increases the quantity demanded. Annual increases in supply resulting from the work projects are considered at 2, 5, and 10%. With a 2% supply increase, a 5% food aid contract, and recipients in the $75 income class, the variables for the equilibrium model are $\Psi = 1.07$, $\Gamma = 1.0275$, $e = -0.90$, and $\epsilon = 0.40$. (Although the shift in production is greater than in the grant case, the increase in domestic production does not result in increase in consumer income as does the food aid. Therefore, values for Γ will be the same as before.) The impact of food aid used in this manner drives prices down by about 3.1% and increases total quantity of food demanded by 5.7%. Since 5.0% of the increase is supplied from food aid, only 0.7% comes from domestic production, resulting in a decrease in income for agricultural producers of about 2.4%. If the supply increase experienced from the work projects drawing labor from the group with annual per capita income around $75 is 5% instead of 2%, the impact is even greater. Prices are driven down by approximately 5.1%, and the net effect on domestic supply is an increase of 2.7%; income to domestic producers falls by about 2.5%. Likewise, if the supply response of the same class of work projects is 10%, the resulting price decline is about 8.3%. With a net domestic supply increase of 6.1%, the resulting income loss for domestic producers is about 2.7%.

For ease of comparison, the alternative impacts of drawing labor from consumer groups with $75, $250, and $450 per capita annual incomes and allocating all or only half of the labor to overhead projects in agriculture with projected increases in domestic productivity of 2, 5, and 10% are summarized in Table 2.6. The impacts on price, domestic supply, and income to agricultural producers are listed by percentage in the table. Scanning across the table, one sees that the negative impact on domestic prices increases as a result of the corresponding shifts in supply without associated shifts in demand. As a result of corresponding price and domestic supply changes, income to agricultural producers decreases as productivity of the work projects increases.

Consistent with theoretical supply and demand relationships, the allocation of only half of the work projects to the agricultural sector would have less negative impact on income to agricultural producers than allocation of all the projects to agriculture. The smaller the work project in agriculture, the smaller the impact on domestic supply, and

TABLE 2.6. **Impact of Work Projects on Agricultural Prices, Supply, and Income**

Income Level of Labor Force	Impact Variable	Expected Supply Increase					
		50% of projects in ag.			100% of projects in ag.		
		2(1)%	5(2½)%	10(5)%	2%	5%	10%
$75	Price	—2.4	—3.4	—5.1	—3.1	—5.1	—8.3
	Supply	0.0	1.0	2.7	0.7	2.7	6.1
	Income	—2.4	—2.4	—2.5	—2.4	—2.5	—2.7
$250	Price	—3.7	—4.9	—6.9	—4.5	—6.9	—10.6
	Supply	—0.2	0.4	1.9	0.0	1.9	5.0
	Income	—3.9	—4.5	—5.1	—4.5	—5.1	—6.1
$450	Price	—4.9	—6.4	—8.7	—5.9	—8.7	—13.1
	Supply	—1.1	—0.3	1.0	—0.6	1.0	3.7
	Income	—6.0	—6.7	—7.8	—6.5	—7.8	—9.9

consequently the smaller the impact on agricultural prices and income.

In summary, the use of P.L. 480 commodities to finance work projects is estimated to have a negative impact on income to agricultural producers ranging from 2.4 to 9.9%, depending on the location and productivity of projects. Domestic supply increases in all cases where 100% of the work projects are in agriculture except where labor comes from the high income group and the work project shifts supply upward by only 2%. For all the other cases the quantity of domestic commodities supplied increases so that if prices were supported for the producer, agricultural income would be maintained or increased. The decline in agricultural income represents a net gain to consumers as the result of lower prices and increased supply of food, and a transfer to nonagricultural sectors if the gain in real income is reallocated to nonfood commodities.

To this point we have considered the source of the labor for work projects only by income level. If all labor comes from agriculture, agricultural income increases by the additional value of food aid. The additional income from the work projects offsets the income loss in all cases where work projects draw labor from the low income group and in most cases where labor is supplied by the medium income group (Table 2.6). Consequently using food aid for work projects in agriculture by hiring labor from the agricultural sector will increase agricultural output, lower food prices, increase total income to the agricultural sector (taking into consideration the value of wages-in-kind), and increase income to the nonagricultural sector. Programming food aid in this manner would improve welfare on a Pareto optimal basis, because welfare would be increased for both agricultural producers and consumers. (Movement toward a Pareto optimum position requires that at least one individual is made better off without anyone else being made worse off.) If labor for the work projects is drawn from the nonagricultural sector, the program does not improve welfare on a Pareto optimal basis so does not necessarily have a net positive effect. Transfer of income from agriculture to nonagriculture has no effect on balance, but the additional food aid has a positive effect on consumers outside agriculture. Determining the net impact in this case involves comparing a gain for one group in the economy with a loss for another group. Although aggregate measures of welfare indicate a gain, it is difficult if not impossible to measure real net gains because of the need to make interpersonal utility comparisons.

ALTERNATIVE MODES OF DISTRIBUTION. Although several alternatives exist for contracting food aid from the United States, the price, production, and income impact of aid on the recipient economy depends on the distribution methods used. These in turn are closely related to the specific consumer group reached and the extent to which productive resources are activated. Under the program approach we have shown that the presence of a differentiated market in India resulted in considerably reducing the price and production impact compared to a situation where food aid commodities are distributed through the open market. We have also presented the impact of food aid on price and production in the recipient economy if a project approach is followed and commodities are distributed to a restricted group of the population. These estimates can be compared with the price and production impact under open market distribution.

Sales on the open market will, of necessity, reach consumers having an income from any source and operating in the market system. With this method it is more difficult to regulate the composition of the recipient group than with the grants and work projects, but techniques such as food stamp plans or other types of regulatory authorization can be used to ascertain the characteristics of the recipients. Another control technique is to distribute the food aid through government regulated shops such as the fair-price shops in India but at competitive market prices.

For analysis of the open market system we will consider three income groups in combination with two levels of investment in agriculture and three levels of return on projects. We will assume that the government does not relieve taxes and consequently does not provide any direct income effect on consumers. On this basis a food aid contract amounting to 5% of present supply combined with reinvestment in

TABLE 2.7. Impact of Sales on Agricultural Prices, Supply, and Income

Income Level of Labor Force	Impact Variable	Expected Supply Increase					
		50% of projects in ag.			100% of projects in ag.		
		2(1)%	5(2½)%	10(5)%	2%	5%	10%
$75	Price	—4.4	—5.4	—7.1	—4.8	—7.1	—10.2
	Supply	—0.9	0.1	1.9	—0.2	1.8	5.3
	Income	—5.3	—5.3	—5.3	—5.0	—5.4	—5.4
$250	Price	—5.2	—6.4	—8.3	—6.0	—8.3	—11.9
	Supply	—1.2	—0.3	1.3	—0.6	1.3	4.3
	Income	—6.3	—6.6	—7.1	—6.5	—7.1	—8.1
$450	Price	—6.3	—7.7	—10.0	—7.2	—10.0	—14.4
	Supply	—1.7	—0.9	0.4	—1.2	0.4	3.1
	Income	—7.9	—8.5	—9.7	—8.4	—9.7	—11.8

projects using labor from the $75 class and resulting in a 2% shift in supply would cause a 4.8% decline in prices and a corresponding 0.2% decline in domestic supply. The resultant loss of income for the agricultural producers would be 5.0% (Table 2.7).

Financing projects in the same way but drawing labor from the $250 class would increase the price decline to 6.0% and the supply reduction to 0.6% for a 6.5% income loss for agricultural producers. Use of labor from the $450 class would cause an even greater decline of 7.2% for prices and 1.2% for supply so that income would fall by 8.4%. Scanning down the other columns of Table 2.7 we find similarities to wage-in-kind projects (Table 2.6). The higher the income level of the group supplying the labor, the greater the negative impact on prices, supply, and income for the agricultural sector. Similarly, scanning across Table 2.7 we find the price impact increases as investment in agricultural projects increases and as productivity of a project increases. Although a declining price level results in movement down the domestic supply curve, the investment in overhead projects results in an upward shift of the supply curve so that domestic supply decreases less with investments in more productive projects. If the projects are productive enough, supply may even be increased.

Distribution of food through open market sales results in similar but stronger effects on the agricultural sector than distribution through work projects. In both types of distribution the price of food usually is driven down and domestic supply forced below preprogram levels. In open market sales the income loss always exceeds 5%, so even if all work projects used labor from the agricultural sector, the total income to the sector would be lower than preprogram levels. Regardless of who received the extra income from the projects, consumers realize improved welfare through lower food prices, and the nonagricultural sector becomes better off than the agricultural sector.

CONCLUSIONS. At the beginning of this chapter we raised the question of whether there is any way to minimize the negative price, production, and income impact on agriculture in recipient countries of food aid. The answer to this question is yes. We can minimize price and production impact by creating a differentiated market for the food aid commodities in the recipient countries. In this context the distribution of food aid commodities through a system of fair-price shops in India is of considerable interest in programming food aid to other recipient countries. As more and more recipient countries show a preference to a program approach of food aid rather than a project approach, the Indian example of fair-price shops can be included as part of the contracts for future food aid. This would raise the real income of the consumers, minimize the negative effects of aid, and increase the beneficial effects. We believe food aid if given on suitable terms can still play an important role in international economic aid, despite the Green Revolution in many recipient countries.

CHAPTER THREE

Terms of Food Aid

INTERNATIONAL AID to developing countries has been in the form of either grants (or grantlike contributions) or loans. While the net capital transfer under grants and grantlike contributions was close to their gross value, the net capital transfer under loans varied according to the terms of aid. The terms of aid (loan component) may be expressed in three dimensions: (1) interest rate, (2) maturity period, and (3) grace period. An increase (decrease) in grace period and maturity period implies softening (hardening) of the terms of aid; an increase (decrease) in interest rate results in hardening (softening) of the terms of aid. The changes in the net capital transfer under loans depend on the hardening or softening of the terms of loan commitments.

An increasing number of donor countries have complied with 1965 Development Assistance Committee (DAC) recommendations for the terms of aid in recent years. Full compliance with 1965 DAC terms of aid recommendations means either that the grant percentage is 70% or more or that all three alternative provisions relating to loans and grants are fulfilled. These alternative provisions are:

1. 81% of total commitments as grants and loans at 3% interest or less.
2. 82% of total commitments as grants and loans with a maturity of 25 years or more.
3. A weighted average grace period of 7 years.

While grace period and maturity period of loans have increased, the interest rates have shown some decline. This situation has led to a softening in the terms of aid (loan component) to developing countries (Table 3.1).

The weighted average grace period for all DAC countries increased from 4.6 years in 1965 to 6.0 years in 1968; the weighted average maturity period increased from 22.6 years in 1965 to 26.0 years in 1968. The interest rates of some donor nations, notably the United Kingdom and Japan, were lower in 1968 than in 1965. However, due to some offsetting increases in the interest rates of other donors, particularly the United States, the weighted average interest rate for all DAC countries remained at the same level in 1968 as in 1965.

TABLE 3.1. Average Terms of Aid in Recent Years

Countries	Weighted Average Grace Period of Loan Commitment (years)				Weighted Average Maturity Period (years)				Weighted Average Interest Rates (%)			
	1965	1966	1967	1968	1965	1966	1967	1968	1965	1966	1967	1968
Australia	(a)	(a)	(a)	(a)	(a)	(a)	(a)	(a)	(a)	(a)	(a)	(a)
Austria	0.9	2.0	3.7	1.9	7.7	9.4	14.6	16.8	5.5	5.4	5.2	5.1
Belgium	4.0	4.3	5.0	6.1	6.2	13.9	18.2	21.9	3.0	2.9	3.2	3.2
Canada	6.3	6.5	4.4	6.9	32.9	34.3	30.9	36.9	3.4	2.4	3.4	2.3
Denmark	2.4	4.2	6.6	7.0	13.7	18.7	24.0	24.9	5.3	0.0	0.0	0.0
France	2.8	2.4	1.8	1.7	16.8	15.3	15.1	17.6	3.7	3.5	3.7	3.7
Germany	3.6	5.6	4.9	5.3	16.9	21.1	19.0	18.0	4.2	3.3	4.3	4.5
Italy	0.7	0.9	1.0	1.7	7.1	10.3	11.9	10.6	4.7	5.0	4.9	4.2
Japan	5.9	6.6	6.7	7.0	12.0	14.1	16.6	18.1	4.4	5.2	4.8	3.7
Netherlands	4.1	5.9	6.3	6.8	23.9	23.6	24.7	29.7	3.5	2.0	3.3	3.8
Norway	6.0	(a)	(a)	5.5	16.0	(a)	(a)	23.0	3.0	(a)	(a)	2.2
Portugal	3.8	4.1	2.2	5.5	21.5	25.4	16.2	22.6	3.8	3.6	4.8	5.6
Sweden	4.8	5.0	6.4	9.6	20.0	20.0	21.4	34.0	2.0	2.0	2.0	1.5
Switzerland	6.0	5.6	(a)	7.7	18.1	16.3	(a)	32.9	4.5	3.8	(a)	2.2
United Kingdom	4.8	6.0	5.5	5.6	22.2	23.9	24.1	24.0	3.3	1.0	1.1	1.0
United States	5.9	6.6	6.7	7.0	27.9	29.3	28.2	30.0	3.3	3.0	3.6	3.6
Total DAC countries	4.6	5.8	5.5	6.0	22.6	25.1	24.0	26.0	3.6	3.1	3.8	3.6

Source: OECD, *Developing World*.
(a). No loans.

The U.S. food aid has been unique from the viewpoint of international indebtedness. Food shipments for local currencies of the recipient countries were treated as grantlike operations by DAC and other international statistics because, except for a small portion of funds retained by the United States for its use, the funds were given back to the recipient governments or private firms in the form of loans and grants. In this sense food aid was augmenting the total aid to developing countries without adding to the debt servicing problems in the recipient countries. However the nature of food aid changed completely with the amendment of P.L. 480 in 1966. This amendment required a progressive shift from local currency sales to long-term dollar sales. Consequently dollar sales have constituted an increasing proportion of total sales under P.L. 480 in recent years (Table 3.2).

This change in the nature of food aid is also reflected in a decline of grants as a percentage of total aid commitments of donor nations, particularly the United States (Table 3.3). Grants as a percentage of total aid commitments by the United States came down from 61.7 in

TABLE 3.2. Sales for Local Currencies and Dollars as a Percentage of All P.L. 480 Sales

	1962	1963	1964	1965	1966	1967	1968
Local currencies	96.7	95.1	92.1	84.2	74.9	72.7	51.9
Dollars	3.3	4.9	7.9	15.8	25.1	27.3	48.1
Total	100.0	100.0	100.0	100.0	100.0	100.0	100.0

Source: OECD, *Developing World.*

1965 to 44.5 in 1968. Grants as a percentage of total aid commitment of all DAC countries came down from 60.9 in 1965 to 51.4 in 1968. These changes in the terms of U.S. food aid have put this aid at par with nonfood aid from the viewpoint of additional debt service obligations.

HARDENING OF TERMS IN AUGMENTING TOTAL AID. The implications of changes in food aid terms for the net inflow of resources to less developed countries (LDCs) can be visualized by looking at the point of zero net aid, even if gross aid remains at the same level during the entire period. As a result of this change the point of zero net aid will be reached much sooner; since food aid has been put at par with nonfood aid in terms of repayment obligations, the recipient countries can weigh the net gain of food aid against nonfood aid by looking at the "grant element" in food aid at the present aid terms.

TABLE 3.3. Grants as a Percentage of Total Aid Commitment

Country	1965	1966	1967	1968
Australia	100.0	100.0	100.0	100.0
Austria	13.8	24.0	29.0	51.4
Belgium	97.9	94.3	94.0	95.2
Canada	54.1	77.0	48.5	75.0
Denmark	70.3	62.5	63.5	57.3
France	79.8	83.1	73.7	71.6
Germany	42.6	41.9	34.2	37.5
Italy	27.8	40.2	19.7	25.2
Japan	37.2	41.5	37.6	61.7
Netherlands	70.8	75.5	71.5	51.5
Norway	95.7	100.0	100.0	92.2
Portugal	28.7	22.7	18.6	20.7
Sweden	88.9	70.7	84.0	75.0
Switzerland	78.2	65.2	100.0	72.5
United Kingdom	55.2	49.7	57.2	46.0
United States	61.7	61.2	56.1	44.5
Total DAC countries	60.9	62.2	56.1	51.4

Source: OECD, *Developing World.*

Dollar Sales and Debt Service Obligations. Extended loan contracts used to finance food aid imports obligate the recipient to reimburse the donor for the value of commodities received and for accumulated interest. As the length of the contract is extended and/or the interest rate increased, the magnitude of payments to service the debt increases proportionately. When a continual flow of aid is financed in this manner, the cumulative value of the annual debt will exceed the value of the new aid at some time during the repayment period for all the positive interest rates.

Consider an agreement to receive a constant amount of food aid X each year on credit terms with repayment beginning at the start of the second year. If the principal payment is a fixed amount per year over a period of N years, the amount of principal payment P due in year n can be written as a function of n and N.

$$P_n = X \frac{n-1}{N} \text{ for } n \leq N + 1 \tag{3.1}$$

The interest payment I can be written as a function of the interest rate r and the sum of the interest on the balance of the loan for each previous year

$$I_n = r \sum_{k=2}^{n} X \left(1 - \frac{k-2}{N} \right) \text{ for } n \leq N + 1 \tag{3.2}$$

using k as an accounting variable. In any given period the total payment C on the debt retirement is equal to the sum of (3.1) and (3.2). This can be expressed as follows:

$$C_n = X \frac{n-1}{N} + r \sum_{k=2}^{n} X \left(1 - \frac{k-2}{N} \right) \text{ for } n \leq N + 1 \tag{3.3}$$

Since this repayment schedule provides for the loan from period one to be liquidated in period $N + 1$, both the principal and interest payment reach a maximum when n equals $N + 1$. Substituting in (3.1), the maximum principal payment is equal to the magnitude of the annual food aid contract:

$$P_{\text{max}} = X \frac{(N+1)-1}{N} = X \frac{N}{N} = X \tag{3.4}$$

Likewise the maximum value for the interest payment is obtained by substituting $N + 1$ for n in the summation, and solving (3.2) we get

$$I_{max} = r \sum_{k=2}^{N+1} X \left(1 - \frac{k-2}{N} \right) = r \, (X) \, \frac{N+1}{2} \qquad (3.5)$$

Given that r and n are positive values, I_{max} is greater than zero, so the value of payment due is greater than the magnitude of the aid received in that period. The point at which the payment exceeds the new contract is defined where the total payment is equal to X (3.6). Equation 3.6 reduces to (3.7) which provides a quadratic equation for the point where payments equal the new contract.

$$C_n = X \, \frac{n-1}{N} + r \, (X) \left[\frac{(n-1) \, (2N - n + 2)}{2N} \right] = X \qquad (3.6)$$

$$\frac{n-1}{N} + r \left[\frac{(n-1) \, (2N - n + 2)}{2N} \right] = 1.0 \qquad (3.7)$$

Solving for n in (3.7) we get

$$- rn^2 + 2Nrn + 3rn + 2n - 2Nr - 2N - 2r - 2 = 0 \qquad (3.8)$$

By using the general quadratic equation formula

$$n = \frac{-b + \sqrt{b^2 - 4ac}}{2a} \qquad (3.9)$$

payments from the recipient country will exceed the gross value of food aid at

$$n = \qquad (3.10)$$
$$\frac{- (2Nr+3r+2) + \sqrt{(2Nr+3r+2)^2 - 4 \, (-r) \, (-2Nr-2N-2r-2)}}{2 \, (-r)}$$

Figures 3.1–3.3 illustrate the point: three repayment schedules —10, 20, and 30 years—are compared using interest rates from 0 to 10%. The grid bases for the figures represent combinations of time (0 to 36

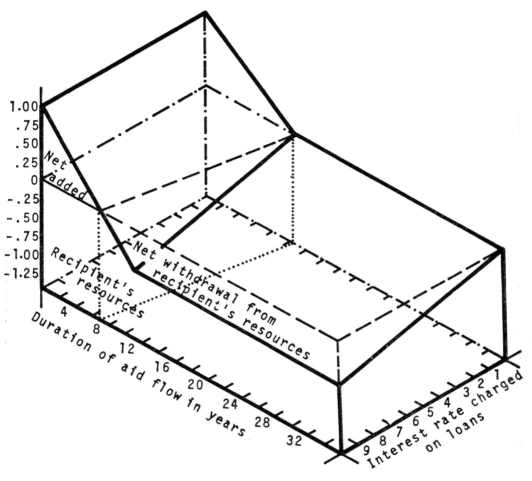

Fig. 3.1. Effect of aid flow duration and interest rates on recipient's net resource position after loan servicing, 10-year repayment schedule.

years) and interest rates (0 to 10%). The vertical distance from each time and interest combination to the surface of the three-dimensional figure indicates the net contribution of aid to the recipient's resources. If the distance is greater than the distance from the base to the zero point on the vertical axis, the contribution is positive; if it is less, the contribution is negative. The period between the time the net aid becomes negative and the maximum value of payments varies according to the length of the repayment period and the interest rate. As the length of

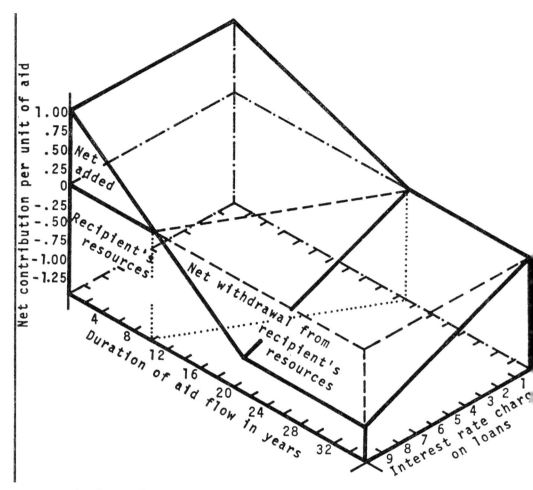

Fig. 3.2. Effect of aid flow duration and interest rates on recipient's net resource position after loan servicing, 20-year repayment schedule.

the repayment schedule increases, the maximum value of payments increases as total interest costs rise, and higher interest rates are positively correlated with higher payments. Using an example of 4% interest on a continual flow of aid over a 20-year period, annual payments to retire the long-term loan equal the annual aid received in about 15.3 years.

Grant Element in Dollar Sales. The concept of grant element measures sacrifice involved in lending the value of food aid at the softer terms compared with the alternative sources of finance. The

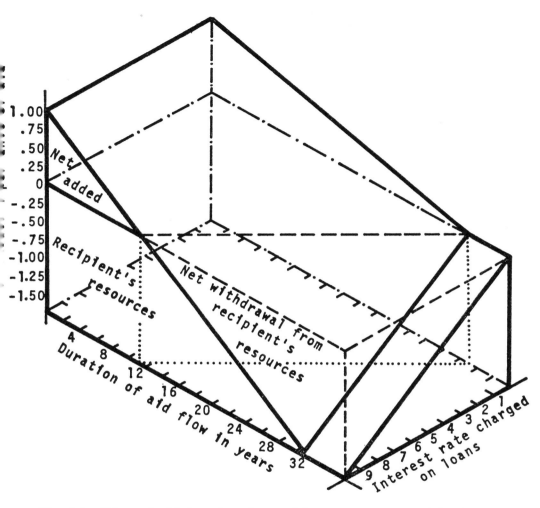

Fig. 3.3. Effect of aid flow duration and interest rates on recipient's net resource position after loan servicing, 30-year repayment schedule.

grant element is worked out by discounting the sum of repayments due under a given loan by a comparative rate of discount and deducting this sum from the face value of the loan. This can be written as follows:[1]

$$\text{Grant element} = L - \sum_{i=1}^{i=T} \frac{C_i + I_i}{\left(1 + \dfrac{q}{100}\right)^i} \qquad (3.11)$$

where

L = face value of the loan
T = maturity period in years
C_i = capital payment due at end of year i
I_i = interest payment due at end of year i
q = comparative rate of discount

Some economists argue that the transportation charges of food shipments, which are paid by the recipient countries, should also be deducted from the grant element to arrive at the net aid component.[2] An idea of the hardening of the terms of P.L. 480 aid can be found in the decline in grant element in recent years, illustrated by recent agreements between India and the United States (Table 3.4).

The percentage of the dollar-repayable portion in P.L. 480 agreements has increased from 20 in the June 1967 agreement to 60 in the October 1969 agreement. Taking this increase into account, the total grant element (aggregate of both dollar-repayable and rupee-repayable portions of loans) has fallen from about 100% to 80.6% in the last agreement. If the rest of the terms continue as they were in the last agreement, it is likely that when 100% of P.L. 480 aid is made repayable in dollars, the grant element will come down to 67.7%. We have used a 10% rate of discount in calculating grant element as is the current practice in the United Nations' studies; with a smaller discount rate the grant element would be further lowered. The grant element would be zero when the interest rate equals the discount rate.

If we take out transportation charges (22.5% on an average), the net aid component comes down from 77.5% to 58.0% in the last agreement. When 100% of P.L. 480 aid becomes repayable in dollars, the net aid component comes down to as low as 45.2% of the face value of the aid.

Pinstrup-Anderson and Tweeten recently worked out lower grant element figures in both local currency–repayable and dollar-repayable food aid.[3] They reached the lower level of grant element by considering three factors: (1) the discounted average and marginal value of aid, (2) an assumed default rate of 10%, and (3) a lower discount rate of 6.5%. These economists presented their calculations of grant element (in dollar-repayable aid) in terms of average per unit of aid and the grant element in the marginal unit of aid. They worked out these calculations by following algebraic formulas:

TABLE 3.4. Grant Element in P.L. 480 Agreements on Long-Term Dollar Credit Sales Basis

| Date of Agreement | Percentage of Repayment in Local Currency | Percentage of Repayment in Dollars | Repayment Terms of Dollar-Payable Portion | | Grant Element of Dollar Credits (%) | Total Grant Element (%) | Total Aid Component (grant element minus transportation charges) (%) |
			Installments	Rate of Interest			
2/20/67	100	...	...	...	...	100.00	77.50
6/24/67	80	20	31 annual repayment installments after 10 years from the last delivery	first 10 years @ 1% next 30 years @ 2½%	75.13	95.03	72.53
9/12/67	80	20	same as above	same as above	75.13	95.03	72.53
12/30/67	80	20	same as above	first 10 years @ 2% next 30 years @ 2½%	69.00	93.80	71.30
12/23/68	60	40	same as above	first 10 years @ 2% next 30 years @ 3%	67.67	87.07	64.57
4/25/68	40	60	same as above	same as above	67.67	80.60	58.10
10/13/69	40	60	same as above	same as above	67.67	80.60	58.10

Note: Discount rate of 10% has been used for arriving at the present value of the loan in the calculations of the grant element.

$$a_1 = AV - \frac{T_i + PV}{QP_w} \, 100 \tag{3.12}$$

$$a_2 = MV - \frac{T_{im} + PV_m}{QP_w} \, 100 \tag{3.13}$$

where

a_1 = average aid component
a_2 = marginal aid component
AV = estimated average value of food aid expressed as a percentage of world market value
MV = estimated marginal value of food aid
T_i = transportation cost payable by the recipient countries
PV = discounted present dollar value of down payments, repayments, and interest payments
Q = quantity of food in physical terms
P_w = world market price in dollars per unit

T_{im} and PV_m refer to the marginal unit.

The average and marginal aid components of the local currency–repayable loans have been worked out as follows:

$$a_i = AV - \frac{T_i + B}{QP_w} \, 100 \tag{3.14}$$

$$a_2 = MV - \frac{T_{im} + MB}{QP_w} \, 100 \tag{3.15}$$

where B is the amount of dollar spending displaced by local currency in the recipient country, and MB is the dollar spending substituted by the local currency obtained at the margin. The empirical results (Table 3.5) show that during 1964–66 the average aid component in local currency–repayable aid varied between 23 and 63% of the face value. The aid component in the marginal unit of aid (local currency–repayable) varied between 47 and 83% of the face value.

In sharp contrast the aid component in dollar-repayable food shipments has been exceedingly small, and in some countries both average and marginal aid components have been negative. The negative

TABLE 3.5. Estimated Value of U.S. Food Aid in Percent of Prevailing World Market Prices and the Aid Components Present for Each of the Survey Countries, 1964–66

Country	Average Value	Marginal Value	Cost of Transportation	Estimated Aid Component							Actual program mix
				20-year credit		40-year credit		Nonconvertible currency			
				average	marginal	average	marginal	average	marginal		
India	90.6	73.1	22.5	1.0	−16.5	8.2	−9.3	53.1	35.6		53.1
Pakistan	...	100.0	16.9	...	16.0	...	23.2	...	74.3		...
Yugoslavia	...	...	14.5	...	...	...	...	...	...		27.2
Brazil	69.0	67.2	17.2	−15.3	−17.1	−8.1	−9.9	33.7	31.9		34.6
Korea, Republic of	68.6	21.4	20.9	−19.6	−6.6	−12.2	0.6	32.5	45.3		24.6
Turkey	65.4	70.6	12.7	−14.4	−9.2	−7.2	−2.0	22.8	28.0		12.9
China, Republic of	70.3	68.4	21.3	−18.1	−20.0	−10.9	−12.8	25.0	23.1		52.9
Israel	85.9	80.5	13.4	5.4	0.0	12.6	7.2	57.5	52.1		22.5
Greece	84.3	77.9	12.9	4.3	−2.1	11.5	5.1	37.1	30.7		31.7
Chile	80.9	78.4	12.9	0.9	−1.6	8.1	5.6	42.0	39.5		57.5
Morocco	100.0	88.3	13.7	19.2	7.3	26.4	14.7	62.3	50.6		62.2
Congo (Kinshasa)	100.0	...	24.1	8.8	...	16.0	...	62.9	...		...
Indonesia	...	...	22.5	...	...	...	...	...	...		...
Colombia	70.9	73.1	13.7	−9.9	−7.7	−2.7	−0.5	29.8	32.0		28.6
Weighted average	79.6	76.9	19.3	−6.8	−9.5	0.4	−2.3	36.7	34.0		43.2

Source: Pinstrup-Anderson and Tweeten, p. 433.

figure of aid component means that recipient countries paid more than the value of food aid when food was priced at world market prices. Pinstrup-Anderson and Tweeten derived their average and marginal values of food aid as a percentage of face value on the basis of a sample survey in 11 countries. They used these values in (3.12)–(3.15) to work out aid components of P.L. 480 shipments. They found the average value was 80% and marginal value 77% and interpret these values as real value of food aid which is equal to cash aid. This additional discounting explains the low values of aid components in Pinstrup-Anderson and Tweeten results.

Even if one may not agree with this discounting procedure, the fact remains that the aid component has become small in dollar-repayable food aid. Food aid on these terms no longer augments the total aid in any significant measure. The pricing of food aid at world market prices has created a large debt servicing burden which will cut through foreign exchange resources in LDCs in coming years.

HARDENING OF TERMS IN LONG-TERM PERSPECTIVE. Total debt service charges of LDCs, which include amortization and interest payments, are already high. Some of these countries have been granted the rescheduling of debt service in the past years to alleviate foreign exchange difficulties. Recently a USAID study[4] made comprehensive projections of debt service charges and debt service ratios (ratio of debt service charges to export earnings) for 17 LDCs. These projections are based on past loans schedules and future inflow of aid. A level of gross aid inflow was assumed for the countries included in the projection. The projections were worked out on the basis of gross aid being constant (at preassigned level) and net aid being constant (gross aid at increasing level so that net aid remains at a preassigned level). Of these two sets of projections, the first set (based on gross aid constancy assumption) is more conservative. Even on the basis of these conservative projections, total debt service charges increase continually at a rapid rate except in Argentina. (Table 3.6).

Table 3.6 shows that the index of debt service charges for India, largest single recipient country, increases from 100 in 1967 to 356 in 1982 and 474 in 1992. The effect of this increase in debt service charges on the debt service ratio should be visualized in terms of the projections of export earnings in the respective countries. Export earnings were first projected at 1960–67 growth rate, 4% growth rate, and 8% growth rate. On the basis of these projections the USAID study worked out the period of rescheduling required in respective countries (Table 3.7).

TABLE 3.6. Debt Service Projections: Gross Aid Constant ($ million)

Country	Interest	Amortization	Total Debt Service	Index of Debt Service	Year
India	147.6	211.1	358.7	100	1967
	324.2	377.6	701.9	196	1972
	428.8	595.2	1,024.0	286	1977
	519.9	758.2	1,278.2	356	1982
	596.1	927.4	1,523.6	425	1987
	649.2	1,050.2	1,699.5	474	1992
Pakistan	44.0	58.1	102.1	100	1967
	116.9	97.4	214.3	210	1972
	169.4	207.4	376.9	369	1977
	211.3	312.6	523.9	513	1982
	240.9	386.4	627.3	614	1987
	261.7	436.8	698.5	684	1992
Brazil	116.1	360.1	476.3	100	1967
	147.0	225.1	372.1	78	1972
	167.0	232.8	399.8	84	1977
	191.5	264.6	456.1	96	1982
	210.7	295.8	506.5	106	1987
	226.0	332.8	558.8	117	1992
Mexico	101.7	353.2	454.9	100	1967
	168.9	289.1	458.0	101	1972
	196.8	422.5	619.3	136	1977
	197.4	463.9	661.3	145	1982
	195.1	442.3	637.4	140	1987
	195.6	442.6	638.2	140	1992
Indonesia	62.7	68.1	130.8	100	1967
	154.0	172.6	326.7	250	1972
	181.2	179.4	360.6	276	1977
	263.8	287.4	551.2	421	1982
	126.1	175.5	301.6	231	1987
	130.9	220.4	351.3	269	1992
Argentina	104.1	351.5	455.6	100	1967
	67.0	188.0	255.0	56	1972
	46.1	116.5	162.5	36	1977
	45.7	108.9	154.6	34	1982
	46.7	111.5	158.1	35	1987
	48.2	120.3	168.4	37	1992
Turkey	46.9	105.4	152.3	100	1967
	52.7	73.8	126.5	83	1972
	65.5	74.7	140.2	92	1977
	80.5	104.1	184.6	121	1982
	93.9	134.8	228.7	150	1987
Chile	37.7	86.1	123.8	100	1967
	73.1	120.7	193.8	157	1972
	94.4	158.9	253.3	205	1977
	107.1	186.7	293.8	237	1982
	114.5	203.6	318.1	257	1987
	119.2	221.4	340.6	275	1992
Colombia	26.3	60.0	86.4	100	1967
	46.1	50.7	96.8	112	1972
	55.5	77.3	132.8	154	1977
	60.3	95.9	156.2	181	1982
	63.1	92.6	155.7	180	1987
	67.3	103.7	171.0	198	1992

TABLE 3.6. *(continued)*

Country	Interest	Amortization	Total Debt Service	Index of Debt Service	Year
Israel	29.9	71.9	101.7	100	1967
	57.4	86.4	143.8	141	1972
	75.1	206.3	281.4	277	1977
	78.9	187.1	266.0	262	1982
	80.4	201.0	281.8	277	1987
	80.2	200.0	280.2	276	1992
Peru	21.0	66.2	87.2	100	1967
	54.1	91.5	145.6	167	1972
	64.5	117.1	181.6	208	1977
	69.0	131.7	200.7	230	1982
	74.4	147.0	221.4	254	1987
	77.4	167.7	245.2	281	1992
Korea	8.1	22.9	31.0	100	1967
	37.7	63.1	100.7	325	1972
	47.3	100.5	147.9	477	1977
	51.6	108.8	160.4	517	1982
	54.0	116.7	170.7	551	1987
	55.6	119.8	175.4	566	1992
Iran	20.7	51.0	71.7	100	1967
	33.9	69.4	103.3	144	1972
	35.7	73.0	108.7	152	1977
	37.6	80.6	118.1	165	1982
	39.4	81.9	121.3	169	1987
	40.9	84.2	125.1	175	1992
Nigeria	13.2	24.9	38.1	100	1967
	40.1	36.0	76.1	200	1972
	51.1	71.4	122.5	322	1977
	54.9	96.8	151.7	398	1982
	55.3	108.7	164.0	430	1987
	54.6	111.1	165.7	435	1992
Tunisia	9.3	27.6	36.9	100	1967
	20.3	37.8	58.1	157	1972
	24.5	45.3	69.8	189	1977
	29.2	51.4	80.6	218	1982
	32.9	54.9	87.8	238	1987
	35.9	60.6	96.5	262	1992
Bolivia	3.4	14.3	17.7	100	1967
	8.4	8.0	16.4	93	1972
	10.8	11.7	22.5	127	1977
	12.3	16.5	28.8	163	1982
	13.1	21.4	34.4	194	1987
	13.2	21.9	35.1	198	1992
Dominican Republic	2.9	11.9	14.8	100	1967
	8.6	6.4	15.0	101	1972
	13.3	19.1	32.4	219	1977
	14.2	26.2	40.4	273	1982
	13.7	23.9	37.6	254	1987
	13.4	23.8	37.1	251	1992
All			2,740.0	100	1967
			3,372.7	123	1972
			4,381.9	160	1977
			5,237.4	191	1982
			5,504.0	201	1987
			n.a.		1992

Source: Frank, Cline, and Gewecke, pp. 20–24.

TABLE 3.7. Debt Rescheduling: Gross Aid Assumption

Country	Years	Export Growth Rate	
		4%	8%
India	1967–92 (26)	1967–92 (26)	1967–92 (26)
Pakistan	1967–92 (26)	1967–92 (26)	1967–92 (26)
Brazil	1967–78 (12)	1967–76 (10)	1967–69 (3)
Mexico	1967–81 (15)	1967–89 (23)	1967–78 (12)
Indonesia	1967–92 (26)	1967–92 (26)	1967–82 (16)
Argentina	1967–68 (2)	1967–69 (3)	1967–68 (2)
Turkey	1968–74 (7)	1968–87 (20)	1968–75 (8)
Chile	. . . (0)	1975–79 (5)	. . . (0)
Colombia	1969–92 (24)	1971, 1973–82 (21)	. . . (0)
Israel	. . . (0)	1968–90 (23)	1973, 1976–77 (3)
Peru	. . . (0)	. . . (0)	. . . (0)
Korea	. . . (0)	1969–92 (24)	1970–78 (9)
Iran	. . . (0)	. . . (0)	. . . (0)
Nigeria	. . . (0)	. . . (0)	. . . (0)
Tunisia	1967–92 (26)	1967–92 (26)	1967–82 (16)
Bolivia	. . . (0)	. . . (0)	. . . (0)
Dominican Republic	1967–92 (17)	. . . (0)	. . . (0)

Source: Frank, Cline, and Gewecke, p. 44.

This study concluded:

India, Pakistan, Indonesia, and Tunisia stand out as countries which are most likely to have persistent debt servicing problems over the next 25 years. This is true regardless of the assumptions concerning gross or net aid and export growth. It should be noted that even repeated reschedulings will not bring the index below the critical value for these countries except if the terms of the rescheduling were extremely generous both with regard to interest and maturities.[5]

India, Pakistan, Indonesia, and Tunisia have been the major recipients of food aid. In this perspective the hardening of the terms of P.L. 480 aid will make the need for rescheduling of debt servicing more important. This need can be illustrated by a discussion of the Indian situation in some detail.

TABLE 3.8. Ratio of Debt Service Payments to Gross Aid Received and Exports in India

Years	Gross Aid Disbursement ($ million)	Total Debt Service Charges ($ million)	Exports ($ million)	Percentage of Col. 3 to Col. 2	Percentage of Col. 3 to Col. 4
1	2	3	4	5	6
1961–62	711	191	1,390	26.86	13.74
1962–63	933	182	1,400	19.50	13.00
1963–64	1,239	209	1,630	16.86	12.82
1964–65	1,520	255	1,750	16.78	14.57
1965–66	1,622	303	1,693	18.68	17.90
1966–67	1,509	363	1,534	24.06	23.66
1967–68	1,570	438	1,673	27.90	26.19
1968–69	1,088	458	1,811	44.12	25.29
1969–70	1,203	506	1,844	42.06	27.44

Source: *Report of Currency and Finance* (Bombay: RBI, 1969–70).

Debt Service Obligations of India. During the entire period of planning (1961–70) the foreign exchange constraint was a limiting factor on the growth of the economy. To relieve this constraint, India received foreign aid of $14,823 million ($17,366 million authorized) up to the end of 1969–70. Debt service charges reached $506 million in 1969–70. This means that foreign exchange availability had to be used only for debt service rather than for crucial and much needed imports. The debt service ratio reached 27% (Table 3.8), far above the level considered critical. A continual increase in debt service ratio reduced the level of net aid availability, which was already reduced due to a lower level of gross aid inflow.

Table 3.8 shows that the debt service ratio rose from 13.74% in 1961–62 to 27.44% in 1969–70. At the same time the proportion of total debt service charges (amortization and interest payments) to gross aid disbursement increased from 26.86% in 1961–62 to 42.06% in 1969–70. This increase in the proportion of total debt service charges to gross aid disbursements indicates the resulting decline in net aid availability to the country from all sources.

The terms of aid (loan component) to India have improved considerably in recent years. The weighted average rate of interest came down to 2.2% in 1967–68 from the peak level of 4.1% in 1964–65 (Table 3.9). The weighted average grace period rose from 5.1 years to 7.4 years, and the maturity period increased from 20.3 years to 30.8 years over the same span of time. However, since P.L. 480 aid has gradually changed from grantlike form to long-term loans, the change will also add to the

TABLE 3.9. Weighted Average of Rate of Interest, Grace Period, and Terms of Maturity of the External Debt

Years	Rate of Interest (%)	Grace Period (years)	Terms of Maturity (years)
1962–63	3.81	5.7	23.9
1963–64	3.75	6.0	24.9
1964–65	4.10	5.1	20.3
1965–66	3.31	5.9	29.3
1966–67	2.39	5.8	27.7
1967–68	2.20	7.4	30.8

Sources: (1) The data above the line pertain to the developing countries as a whole taken from "Foreign Aid: A Symposium Survey and an Appraisal," Indian Council of Current Affairs, p. 512.
(2) The data below the line have been worked out from the aid authorized to India (source by source and loan by loan).

debt service obligations. The dollar-repayable portion of P.L. 480 aid to India was $40.74 million in 1967–68, $80.00 million in 1968–69, and $96.69 million in 1969–70. Since India has been able to stop P.L. 480 imports from the year 1971–72, the amortization and interest payment will continue up to the year 2010 (on the basis of existing dollar-repayable aid under P.L. 480).

PRICING OF FOOD AID. Economists have become concerned about the erosion of the aid component in dollar-repayable food shipments. This concern has led them to examine alternative price levels (lower than world market prices) of food shipments that would preserve the usefulness of food aid without additional costs to the United States. Pinstrup-Anderson and Tweeten estimated that the cost of dollar-repayable aid (both with 20- and 40-year repayment stipulations) is negative to the United States. The net costs have been estimated as "(a) the savings that the United States could have realized by reducing production by the amount of food exported under aid programs, i.e., revenue foregone by maintaining the food aid programs, plus (b) transportation costs on food aid payable by the donor country, less (c) the present value of the disbursements made by the aid recipients."[6]

In this situation the pricing of food shipments at world market rates causes unduly high repayment obligations, and Pinstrup-Anderson and Tweeten suggested that

the repayment of food aid be based on the revenue foregone by the donor country by allocating the commodities to food aid rather than to the best alternative use, e.g., production control. This would preclude a net reverse transfer of resources. Furthermore, the total social gain would be obtained by the aid recipients. The real cost to the donor country would be limited to the difference between the interest charged on the credit and the opportunity cost of capital.[7]

Heady, Mayer, and Madsen recently worked out more comprehensive estimates of prices charged for dollar-repayable food shipments that would not cause any additional expenditure over and above what would otherwise have been incurred on production control in the absence of aid.[8] Since different types of land retirement policies (instrument for the production control) have different costs associated with them, the estimated price per unit also varies accordingly, and the

TABLE 3.10. **Net Cost for Food Aid, Assuming the United States Employs a Long-Range Land Retirement Program with No Limits on Retirement in Any Production Area**

Recipient Country or Area	Level of P.L. 480 Shipments[a]						
	1	2	3	4	5	6	7
Wheat ($ per bu)							
Weighted average	1.40	1.60	1.71	1.74	1.80	1.89	2.01
Brazil	1.33	1.53	1.64	1.67	1.73	1.82	1.96
Morocco	1.35	1.55	1.66	1.69	1.75	1.84	1.98
India-Pakistan	1.41	1.61	1.72	1.75	1.81	1.90	2.04
Turkey	1.40	1.60	1.70	1.73	1.79	1.88	2.03
Korea	1.38	1.58	1.69	1.72	1.78	1.87	2.01
Food grains ($ per bu)[b]							
Average	1.57	1.58	1.59	1.61	1.67	1.68	1.68
Mexico	1.42	1.44	1.44	1.46	1.52	1.53	1.53
Chile	1.58	1.59	1.60	1.62	1.68	1.69	1.69
Tunisia	1.51	1.53	1.53	1.55	1.61	1.62	1.62
Sudan	1.61	1.63	1.63	1.66	1.72	1.72	1.73
India-Pakistan	1.58	1.59	1.60	1.62	1.68	1.69	1.69
Israel	1.52	1.54	1.54	1.57	1.63	1.64	1.64
Korea	1.54	1.56	1.56	1.58	1.64	1.65	1.65
Cotton (¢ per lb of lint)							
Average	20.0	20.6	20.6	21.5	22.2	22.8	25.5
Chile	20.1	20.6	20.6	21.5	22.2	22.8	25.5
Congo	20.1	20.7	20.7	21.6	22.3	22.9	25.6
India-Pakistan	20.1	20.6	20.7	21.5	22.2	22.8	25.6
Korea-Taiwan	20.0	20.6	20.6	21.5	22.2	22.8	25.5

Source: Heady, Mayer, and Madsen, p. 255.
a. Quantities are: million bu of wheat, million tons of food grains, million bales of cotton.

Wheat	75.0	150.0	225.0	300.0	375.0	425.0	525.0
Food grains	1.5	3.0	4.5	6.0	7.5	9.0	10.5
Cotton	1.0	2.0	3.0	4.0	5.0	6.0	7.0

b. Food grain price is per bushel of corn or equivalent nutritive value of other food grain.

optimal price levels vary according to the level of shipment. To incorporate the effects of these combinations of land retirement policies and levels of shipments under aid to different countries, they devised a parametric programming model. The model included 150 producing regions, 31 consuming regions, and 3 commodities. The net costs were worked out on the basis of three alternative land retirement policies and seven alternative levels of shipments. The three alternative land retirement policies were (1) long-range land retirements with no restrictions, (2) long-range land retirement with restrictions, and (3) annual land retirement with direct payment programs. The seven levels of shipments are presented in the note on Table 3.10. The empirical results are presented in Table 3.10, 3.11, and 3.12, which show that the net cost of

TABLE 3.11. Net Cost for Food Aid, Assuming the United States Employs a Long-Range Land Retirement Program with 50% Limit on Retirement in Any Producing Area

Recipient Country or Area	Level of P.L. 480 Shipments[a]						
	1	2	3	4	5	6	7
Wheat ($ per bu)							
Weighted average	1.29	1.34	1.47	1.59	1.59	1.61	1.71
Brazil	1.22	1.27	1.40	1.52	1.52	1.54	1.63
Morocco	1.24	1.29	1.42	1.54	1.54	1.56	1.66
India-Pakistan	1.30	1.35	1.48	1.60	1.60	1.62	1.72
Turkey	1.29	1.34	1.47	1.59	1.59	1.61	1.70
Korea	1.28	1.32	1.45	1.57	1.57	1.59	1.69
Food grains ($ per bu)[b]							
Average	1.43	1.46	1.48	1.49	1.56	1.56	1.57
Mexico	1.28	1.32	1.33	1.34	1.41	1.41	1.42
Chile	1.44	1.47	1.49	1.50	1.57	1.57	1.58
Tunisia	1.37	1.40	1.42	1.43	1.50	1.50	1.51
Sudan	1.48	1.51	1.52	1.53	1.61	1.61	1.61
India-Pakistan	1.44	1.47	1.49	1.50	1.57	1.57	1.58
Israel	1.39	1.42	1.44	1.44	1.52	1.52	1.52
Korea	1.40	1.43	1.45	1.46	1.53	1.53	1.54
Cotton (¢ per lb of lint)							
Average	18.9	20.0	20.0	20.6	20.6	21.4	23.4
Chile	18.9	20.1	20.1	20.7	20.7	21.44	23.5
Congo	19.0	20.1	20.1	20.7	20.7	21.5	23.5
India-Pakistan	18.9	20.1	20.1	20.7	20.7	21.4	23.5
Korea-Taiwan	18.9	20.0	20.0	20.6	20.6	21.4	23.4

Source: Heady, Mayer, and Madsen, p. 257

a. Quantities are: million bu of wheat, million tons of food grains, million bales of cotton.

Wheat	75.0	150.0	225.0	300.0	375.0	425.0	525.0
Food grains	1.5	3.0	4.5	6.0	7.5	9.0	10.5
Cotton	1.0	2.0	3.0	4.0	5.0	6.0	7.0

b. Food grain price is per bushel of corn or equivalent nutritive value of other food grain.

TABLE 3.12. Net Cost for Food Aid, Assuming the United States Employs Annual Land Retirement and Direct Payment Programs for Wheat, Food Grains, and Cotton

Recipient Country or Area	Level of P.L. 480 Shipments[a]						
	1	2	3	4	5	6	7
	Wheat ($ per bu)						
Weighted average	.08	.50	.87	1.05	1.13	1.27	1.31
Brazil	.00	.42	.79	.97	1.05	1.19	1.23
Morocco	.02	.44	.81	.99	1.07	1.21	1.25
India-Pakistan	.09	.51	.89	1.06	1.14	1.28	1.32
Turkey	.05	.54	.84	1.02	1.10	1.24	1.28
Korea	.05	.57	.84	1.02	1.10	1.24	1.28
	Food grains ($ per bu)[b]						
Average	1.08	1.10	1.15	1.17	1.32	1.34	1.34
Mexico	.93	.95	1.01	1.03	1.17	1.19	1.19
Chile	1.09	1.10	1.16	1.18	1.32	1.34	1.34
Tunisia	1.02	1.04	1.10	1.12	1.26	1.28	1.28
Sudan	1.13	1.14	1.20	1.22	1.36	1.38	1.38
India-Pakistan	1.09	1.11	1.16	1.18	1.33	1.35	1.35
Israel	1.04	1.05	1.11	1.13	1.27	1.29	1.29
Korea	1.05	1.07	1.12	1.14	1.29	1.31	1.31
	Cotton (¢ per lb of lint)						
Average	13.8	16.8	17.2	17.2	17.7	18.2	19.2
Chile	13.8	16.8	17.2	17.2	17.7	18.2	19.2
Congo	13.8	16.8	17.2	17.3	17.8	18.2	19.2
India-Pakistan	13.8	16.8	17.2	17.2	17.7	18.2	19.2
Korea-Taiwan	13.7	16.7	17.1	17.2	17.7	18.2	19.1

Source: Heady, Mayer, and Madsen, p. 259.

a. Quantities are: million bu of wheat, million tons of food grains, million bales of cotton.

Wheat	75.0	150.0	225.0	300.0	375.0	425.0	525.0
Food grains	1.5	3.0	4.5	6.0	7.5	9.0	10.5
Cotton	1.0	2.0	3.0	4.0	5.0	6.0	7.0

b. Food grain price is per bushel of corn or equivalent nutritive value of other food grains.

shipment under P.L. 480 dollars increases with the increase in the level of shipment under all three types of land retirement programs considered. The net costs are much smaller for all levels of shipments under annual land retirement programs and direct payments compared with long-range land retirements both with and without restrictions. On the basis of these costs the guidelines for pricing P.L. 480 commodities were evolved as follows:

$$\frac{\text{estimated net opportunity cost}}{\text{gross CCC cost for commodities}} = \text{pricing coefficient}$$

where gross CCC (Commodity Credit Corporation) costs are the gross value of commodities shipped (U.S. market prices) plus the transporta-

TABLE 3.13. Ratio (in percent) of Net Cost to Gross CCC Costs for Shipments of Wheat, Food Grains, and Cotton during 1966–68 under Alternative Supply Control Programs

Type of Land Retirement Program	Level of P.L. 480 Shipments[a]						
	1	2	3	4	5	6	7
	Wheat						
Long-range retirement No restrictions	60.9	69.6	74.3	75.7	78.3	82.2	87.4
Long-range retirement 50% restrictions	56.1	58.3	63.9	69.1	69.1	70.0	74.3
Annual land retirement Direct payments	3.5	21.7	37.8	45.7	49.1	55.2	57.0
	Food grains						
Long-range retirement No restrictions	81.3	81.9	82.4	83.4	86.5	87.0	87.0
Long-range retirement 50% restrictions	74.1	75.6	76.7	77.2	80.8	80.8	81.3
Annual land retirement Direct payments	56.0	57.0	59.6	60.6	68.4	69.4	69.4
	Cotton						
Long-range retirement No restrictions	74.6	76.9	76.9	80.2	82.8	85.1	95.1
Long-range retirement 50% restrictions	70.5	74.6	74.6	76.9	76.9	79.8	87.3
Annual land retirement Direct payments	51.5	62.7	64.2	64.2	66.0	67.9	71.6

Source: Heady, Mayer, and Madsen, p. 261.

Note: Gross CCC costs in 1966–68 are $2.30 per bushel of wheat, $1.93 per bushel of food grains, and 26.8 cents per pound of cotton (Table 3.11).

a. Quantities are: million bu of wheat, million tons of food grains, million bales of cotton.

Wheat	75.0	150.0	225.0	300.0	375.0	425.0	525.0
Feed grains	1.5	3.0	4.5	6.0	7.5	9.0	10.5
Cotton	1.0	2.0	3.0	4.0	5.0	6.0	7.0

tion charges borne by CCC.[9] The pricing coefficient provides the estimate of appropriate prices to be charged under P.L. 480 (at various aid levels in respective countries). The estimates of the pricing coefficient are presented in Table 3.13.

These estimates have also been worked out for all three types of land retirement programs and seven levels of P.L. 480 shipments. Table 3.13 shows that even with the domestic policy of long-range land retirement with no restrictions the estimated prices are considerably lower than the world market prices. In actual practice the production control policy comprises all three types of land retirement policies in some combination, and the prices of P.L. 480 commodities can be kept considerably lower than at present. Since P.L. 480 commodities have been priced on the basis of world market prices, the recovery rate (net return to the United States from food aid) has increased considerably from P.L. 480 shipments and at the same time reduced the net component in shipments to very low levels.

The crucial question is whether we can still preserve the usefulness of food aid as a tool in international development with present repayment terms. The question is categorically answered by the estimates of net costs to the donor country over and above what it would have cost to implement land retirement programs to control production. These estimates show that food aid can be priced at considerably lower levels with no additional cost to the United States. This plan would prevent a reverse inflow of resources from LDCs to the donor countries (as is the case now), and at the same time the aid component of food and fiber shipments would be increased. P.L. 480 shipments should not be included in aid at the present level of pricing and repayment terms.

CHAPTER FOUR

Counterpart Funds

S H I P M E N T S of food under P.L. 480 Title I have created
a financial counterpart in the form of sale proceeds. These proceeds are referred to as "counterpart funds." The problems
raised by these counterpart funds have created a great deal of interest
and concern in both donor and recipient countries.[1] The nature of
counterpart fund operations is such that these funds will continue to be
generated up to the end of the century. The U.S. authorities in the recipient countries are beset with large amounts of past accumulations and
a continuous flow of surplus local currency funds. Some economists have
charged these funds with having an inflationary impact on the recipient's
economy.[2]

The primary objective of this study is to examine the inflationary implications of P.L. 480 counterpart funds in a long-term perspective,
concentrating on the time when imports come to an end. To orient this
analysis, we have examined the inflationary implications of the counterpart funds during the years when food imports were continuing. The
fresh accruals of sale proceeds (in local currencies) have already come
to an end in most of the recipient countries because of the shift of aid
from Title I to Title IV, but the counterpart funds will continue to grow
with loan repayments and interest payments for a long time to come. We
have focused this analysis mainly on India, which has been a major recipient of aid and also faces one of the largest accumulations of local
currencies in the U.S. accounts.

INFLATIONARY IMPLICATIONS. The allegation of inflationary
implications of P.L. 480 counterpart funds has been based primarily on an analysis of complex bookkeeping entries in the
budget papers of the recipient countries. Most participants in the controversy have tended to treat any change in money supply resulting from
the use of counterpart funds in once-only transactions as necessarily having a corresponding effect on prices. In other words, any expansionary,
neutral, or contractionary effects of P.L. 480 on money supply are interpreted as having an automatic inflationary, neutral, or deflationary impact on prices.[3] This interpretation of a change in money caused by
P.L. 480 completely ignores the fact the P.L. 480 aid also leads to an

inflow of real goods into the recipient's economy. External food availability in fact provides an opportunity to increase investments to more than those represented by sale proceeds alone without concurrent price change.[4] The changes in money supply alone cannot be interpreted as inflationary. The contention that P.L. 480 counterpart fund operation causes an increase in existing money stock is based on two implicit conditions.

1. A Necessary Condition: The actual disbursement of counterpart funds for development projects, U.S. uses, and Cooley loans must be equal to the realization of sale proceeds from the public, or

$$\Delta I_g + \Delta U = \Delta S_p$$

where I_g is government investment expenditure, U is U.S. and Cooley fund withdrawals, and S_p is the amount of sale proceeds.

2. A Sufficiency Condition: The equality between accrual of the sale proceeds and their disbursement must hold within the same time period. (Because all the operations are routed through the budget of the recipient countries, time period is taken to be one financial year.)

$$\Delta I_g{}^{t=1} + \Delta U^{t=1} = \Delta S_p{}^{t=1}$$

The nonfulfillment of the sufficiency condition is the crux of the entire controversy over the expansionary impact of P.L. 480 counterpart funds on the money supply. However, as seen in the analysis that follows, nonfulfillment of the sufficiency condition has different effects in a situation of *continuous inflow* of real aid than it does in the event of *once-only inflow* of aid. There are many procedural aspects of P.L. 480 shipments that tend to create time lags between the arrival of food shipments and the disbursement of counterpart funds. These are illustrated with reference to India in the analysis that follows.

Procedural Aspects. A number of financial transactions are involved in P.L. 480 aid. As soon as commodities arrive at Indian ports, the Government of India (GOI) must pay the U.S. Embassy account for the P.L. 480 food and fibers in rupee terms. (Before the amendment of October 8, 1964, 50% of freight charges were also paid in rupees; since that date the entire freight charges are borne in dollars). Until May 1960, the U.S. Embassy account was held in the State Bank of India (SBI); later it was transferred to the Reserve Bank of India (RBI). The accumulated unused funds in the U.S. Embassy account were transferred to the RBI in a number of agreed-upon installments.[5] In the pre-1960 procedure, P.L. 480 counterpart funds were initially invested in government securities pending withdrawals. This procedure increased the credit ratio of the SBI and thereby the money supply; it also overstated the bank credit to the government sector.[6]

Under the new procedure, however, the RBI invests these funds in the special securities of the GOI. Eventually these special securities are redeemed to meet the final disbursement demand arising out of the allocations of funds for the loans and grants to the GOI, for Cooley loans, and for U.S. uses. Before the final disbursement can take place some technical formalities have to be completed. Each P.L. 480 agreement between India and the United States must first be followed by a loan agreement for the earmarked amount. Subsequently, several project agreements must be entered into between the GOI and the U.S. authorities. Delays in completion of these technical formalities have led to the emergence of time lags between accruals and use of counterpart funds— time lags not only with funds earmarked for loans and grants to the GOI and loans for Cooley uses but also with funds meant for use by the United States. In fact the rate of increase in actual withdrawals to funds for U.S. uses is much slower than the rate of increase in funds earmarked for this purpose.

P.L. 480 TRANSACTIONS. To analyze the impact of time lags between accrual and disbursement of counterpart funds, P.L. 480 transactions are first isolated from other banking sector transactions with the government sector. We will term this "isolation assumption," and it will be relaxed later in the analysis. With this framework in mind, we can divide the operations connected with P.L. 480 into three phases: (1) payment for P.L. 480 imports by the GOI and investment of these funds for the United States by the RBI in the GOI special securities, (2) sale of food grains to the public, and (3) final disbursement of counterpart funds for the earmarked uses.

First Phase: Let us assume that we have isolated P.L. 480 transactions from the other budgetary transactions so we can proceed with zero budgetary receipts. There is of course some time lapse in the distribution process before the sale proceeds can actually be recovered, even though the payment to the U.S. Embassy account has to be made as soon as the imported commodities arrive at various ports. So if we observe the conventional budgetary practice in India, the GOI has to borrow from the RBI by issuing *ad hocs* to match the amount. (*Ad hocs* are the treasury bills issued by the GOI to the RBI for temporary credit.) This arrangement means an increase in the financial assets of the banking system and an increase in the money supply. Under the new procedure the deposits in the U.S. Embassy account have to be invested immediately in the special securities, and the earlier increase in financial assets is nullified except for any incidental charges. The result is two bookkeeping entries at RBI but no change in total money supply.

Second Phase: The commodities are sold to the public and the sale proceeds are realized. Under the isolation assumption, these proceeds will create positive cash balances of GOI with the RBI. Consequently the nonmonetary liabilities of the banking system will increase, which will lead to a contraction in the money supply. A small part of the contraction (incidental charges) will go to neutralize the earlier expansion of money supply. The remaining contraction will result in a deflationary impact until GOI spends its cash balances.

Third Phase: The counterpart funds are disbursed for all earmarked uses—loans and grants to the GOI, Cooley loans, and U.S. uses. The special securities are first monetized for these withdrawals and then withdrawals are made for the earmarked uses. These expenditures offset the contraction in the money supply outlined in the second phase.

If all phases of P.L. 480 operations fall within one financial year (i.e., if the necessary as well as the sufficiency conditions are fulfilled), the impact of these operations on money supply will be neutral and the agreed-upon projects will be financed without adding to existing money stock in the economy. If these conditions are not met, monetary expansion may be generated. To see the effect of nonfulfillment of the sufficiency condition, let us take an illustration in which the third phase is not fully completed within one financial year. The illustration will consider a once-only import transaction.

In the following hypothetical example the value of food and fiber imports is assumed to be Rs 100 crores with Rs 8 crores taken as incidental charges (1 crore = 10 million Rs). Assuming there is no subsidy, the net impact of Phases I and II is a contraction of money supply by Rs 100 crores (Table 4.1). We are assuming that only Rs 50 crores are finally withdrawn from this amount by the U.S. Embassy for meeting the claims of GOI (Rs 20 crores as loans and Rs 20 crores for grants), Cooley loans (Rs 5 crores), and Embassy expenditures (Rs 5 crores) in the initial year. The remaining amount of Rs 50 crores is

TABLE 4.1. Impact of Phases I and II of P.L. 480 Transactions in Disaggregative Terms in First Year

Transaction	Changes in Financial assets		Changes in Nonmonetary liabilities		Net Bank Credit to Government	Changes in Money Supply
	Asset	Amount	Asset	Amount		
			(Rs crores)			
1. Payment for P.L. 480 food to RBI	Ad hoc treasury bills	100			108	108
For meeting the incidentals		8				
2. U.S. Embassy investment in special securities by RBI			Govt. cash balances	100	−100	−100
Net impact of Phase I (transactions 1 & 2)	Ad hocs	8			8	8
1. Sale of imported food grains and recovery of proceeds for fibers from private parties				108	−108	−108
Net impact of Phase II				108	−108	−108
Net impact of Phases I and II				100	−100	−100

Source: Adapted from "Effect of the United States Commodity Assistance to India on Money Supply," *Reserve Bank of India Bulletin* 17 (Jan. 1963):20–30. Incidental charges of handling and distribution have been brought into the picture.

withdrawn in the second year. The impact of this phase can be seen in Table 4.2.

In the first year a contraction of Rs 50 crores remains in the money supply which is neutralized in the second year, but the total money supply will decline in the first year. In the second year the situation will be reversed because expenditures will not be matched by surplus food. The nonfulfillment of the sufficiency condition results in monetary contraction or expansion at different times under the isolation assumption. In a situation of continual imports, however, even the expansionary impact as depicted in the second year may or may not result, since the expansionary impact of withdrawals of last year's accumulated funds may be offset by the current year's imports. With continual imports of approximately constant magnitude, no substantial expansionary impact is likely to result. If all three phases of counterpart fund operations are completed in one financial year, the possibilities for expansionary impacts do not arise.

TABLE 4.2.   Impact of Final Disbursement of P.L. 480 Counterpart Funds on Money Supply in First and Second Years

	Changes in				Net Bank Credit to Government	Change in Money Supply
	Financial assets		Nonmonetary liabilities			
Transaction	Asset	Amount	Asset	Amount		
					(Rs crores)	
	First Year					
Net impact of Phases I and II	...	...	Government balance	100	—100	—100
Disbursement of counterpart funds in first year	...	...	Government cash balance	—50	50	50
Net impact of Phases I, II, and III in first year	...	...		50	—50	—50
	Second Year					
Net impact of Phases I, II, and III in second year	...	...		50	—50	—50
Disbursement of counter part funds in second year	...	...		—50	50	50
Net impact of P.L. 480 operations in first and second years	...	...		0	0	0

OTHER BUDGETARY TRANSACTIONS. So far the analysis of the impact of P.L. 480 transactions on money supply has been conducted in isolation from other budgetary transactions. The isolation assumption may now be relaxed. With the relaxation of the isolation assumption, the P.L. 480 transactions form part of the budget of the GOI. Within the earlier framework of analysis the contractionary effect in the first year and the expansionary inflationary impact in the second year may or may not obtain, depending on the surplus and the deficit of the GOI budget as a whole. Since the budget in India has always been in deficit, critics allege a double use of P.L. 480 counterpart funds: (1) in the form of the sale proceeds and (2) in the form of the actual disbursement of the counterpart funds.[7] This double use forms the basis of the contention that P.L. 480 counterpart funds have an expansionary impact on the money supply.

We can show that the argument about double use of funds is fallacious in the real case of continual importations. In the continual process of imports under P.L. 480, the problem of redeeming the past securities, because of time lags, arises only when current accruals fall short of current disbursements of funds in any financial year. Here too the lagged disbursements for loans and grants to the GOI do not add to a surplus or a deficit. Only the lagged withdrawals for U.S. uses and Cooley funds add to the deficit if the fresh accruals of sale proceeds in any year fall short of such withdrawals. (We have presented entries relating to P.L. 480 operation in the GOI budget in Appendix B to aid in understanding the discussion.)

Continual Imports. Some of the logical steps of earlier analysis—the initial creation of *ad hocs* to pay for P.L. 480 imports and subsequent investment in special securities by the Reserve Bank—became redundant in view of their accounting significance only. Therefore, we can begin the analysis with the actual realization of the sale proceeds. Let us assume that the sale proceeds are equal to the economic cost (initial payment to U.S. Embassy + incidentals). In real practice there are losses on the state trading account (an account of the GOI budget that presents the payments and receipts from government operations in food grains) because of a subsidy to the price in fair-price shops. The sale proceeds are earmarked for the four types of uses. Let X_{1i}, X_{2i}, X_{3i}, and X_{4i} represent the loans to GOI, grants to GOI, U.S. uses, and Cooley loans respectively in the period i. (Period represents a financial year, i.e., April–March.) Also let

$$X_{1i} + X_{2i} + X_{3i} + X_{4i} = Y_i \qquad (4.1)$$

wherein Y_i is the sale proceeds out of P.L. 480 imports. Let p_{1i}, p_{2i}, p_{3i}, and p_{4i} be the proportion of the fresh accruals of the sale proceeds earmarked for loans to GOI, grants to GOI, U.S. uses, and Cooley loans.

$$X_{ki} = p_{ki}Y_i \qquad (K = 1, 2, 3, 4) \qquad (4.2)$$

The whole of the earmarked amount is not actually disbursed in the same period. Let C_{ki} be the proportion actually disbursed for the earmarked purpose out of X_{ki}. Officially undisbursed funds continue to remain invested in special securities. Besides this amount, the loan repayment and interest payments by GOI and the funds transferred from SBI to RBI also remain invested in special securities. By the end of the first period the amount invested in the special securities is:

$$S_1 = \sum_{k=1}^{4} X_{k1} (1 - C_{k1}) + (P_1 + M_1 + T_1)$$
$$+ (R_1 + O_1) + R_1 \qquad (4.3)$$

where S_1 is the investment in special securities, P_1 is the loan repayment by GOI, M_1 is the interest payment by GOI, and T_1 is the transfer from SBI to RBI. R_1 and O_1 represent the Cooley fund principal repayment and interest payments in special securities. In the first period $P_1 = 0$ and $M_1 = 0$, because the terms of the loan repayments state that they start after a certain period from the date of the first disbursement of the loan. Similarly, $T_1 = 0$ because the transfers started as late as 1960, after the change in procedure for holding the funds. In the first period $R_1 = 0$ and $O_1 = 0$ because these repayments and interest payments started at a very late stage.

Net Budgetary Support in First Period. The net budgetary support, B_1, which is an index of the noninflationary finance mobilized in the first year,[8] can be written as:

$$B_1 = X_{11}C_{11} + X_{21}C_{21} - (P_1 + M_1 + T_1 + R_1)$$
$$+ \sum_{k=1}^{4} X_{ki} (1 - C_{ki}) + (P_1 + M_1 + T_1)$$
$$+ (R_1 + O_1) + R_1 - L_1 \qquad (4.4)$$

L_1 has been introduced to take into account the loss on the state trading account (economic cost minus sale proceeds) which arises from the subsidized sale price of imported grain through the fair-price shops. In simplified terms, it comes to:

$$B_1 = X_{11} + X_{21} + X_{31}(1 - C_{31}) + X_4 (1 - C_{41})$$
$$+ (R_1 + O_1) - L_1 \qquad (4.5)$$

In economic terms this means that in the first year the amounts earmarked for loans and grants (both actually disbursed and not disbursed in the form of investment in special securities) and the undrawn amount for U.S. uses and Cooley funds are used as budgetary receipts in the first period itself. Losses on the state trading account go to reduce the net budgetary support.

Net Budgetary Support in Second Period. Out of the earmarked amounts there will be some leftovers from the second period's actual accruals. As in the first year these leftovers will go to swell the investments in special securities; at the same time there will be some lagged withdrawals from the leftover funds of the first year for all the earmarked purposes, and these will reduce the investment in special securities. Therefore, the net increase in investment in special securities at the end of the second period will be:

$$S_2 = \sum_{k=1}^{4} X_{k2}(1 - C_{k2}) + (P_2 + M_2 + T_2)$$

$$+ (R_2 + O_2) + R_2 - \sum_{k=1}^{4} d_{k1} \qquad\qquad (4.6a)$$

where d_{k1} represents the lagged withdrawal of the earmarked funds from X_{k1}. We note that:

$$0 \leqq d_{ki} \leqq X_{ki}(1 - C_{ki}) \qquad\qquad (k = 1, 2, 4)$$

and

$$d_{3i} \leqq X_{ki}(1 - C_{ki}) + (P_i + M_i + T_i) + (R_i + O_i)$$
$$+ R_i \qquad (k = 3) \qquad\qquad (4.6b)$$

Finally the support of P.L. 480 counterpart funds to the budget of the GOI can be written as:

$$B_2 = (X_{12}C_{12} + d_{11}) + (X_{22}C_{22} + d_{22}) - (P_2 + M_2 + T_2)$$

$$- R_2 + \sum_{k=1}^{4} X_{k2} (1 - C_{k2}) + (P_2 + M_2 + T_2)$$

$$+ (R_2 + O_2) + R_2 - \sum_{k=1}^{4} d_{k2} - L_2 \qquad\qquad (4.7)$$

In simplified terms it means:

$$B_2 = X_{12} + X_{22} + X_{32} (1 - C_{32}) + X_{42} (1 - C_{42})$$
$$+ (R_2 + O_2) - (d_{31} + d_{41}) - L_2 \qquad\qquad (4.8)$$

This holds true until the imports continue under P.L. 480 program (i.e., $Y_i > 0$). Thus, more generally, in any period i we have the net budgetary support as:

$$B_i = X_{1i} + X_{2i} + X_{3i}(1 - C_{3i}) + X_{4i}(1 - C_{4i})$$
$$+ (R_i + O_i) - (d_{3i} + d_{4i}) - L_i \qquad\qquad (4.9)$$

When P.L. 480 Imports Cease. If the imports cease, Y_i (fresh realizations of sale proceeds) will become zero in the ith period. Then

X_{1i}, X_{2i}, X_{3i}, X_{4i}, and L_i will be zero. But O_i, R_i, d_{3i}, and d_{4i} will not vanish; hence our general form of the equation will be reduced to:

$$B_i = (R_i + O_i) - (d_{3i} + d_{4i}) \tag{4.10}$$

Since $(R_i + O_i) < (d_{3i} + d_{4i})$, it is the lagged withdrawal of these U.S. and Cooley funds that will not be matched by the grain flows from abroad. We will take up the problems associated with these portions of counterpart fund accruals in the next section.

Net Support. A continual budgetary deficit has existed in India from 1956–57 to 1968–69 except for the year 1960–61. To arrive at a conclusion about the effect of P.L. 480 operations, we need to see the values of the net support of these operations to the budget. If the net support is positive (and total money supply is reduced), we can say with certainty that P.L. 480 counterpart funds have helped to reduce the budgetary deficit. In other words, these counterpart funds have supported larger GOI expenditures without resorting to additional budgetary deficit. Since imports of agricultural products under P.L. 480 have been positive between 1956–57 and 1968–69, the net support has been positive.

The net support of P.L. 480 aid to the budget of GOI has ranged between Rs 23.12 crores and Rs 370.01 crores (Table 4.3). In no period has the budgetary support of P.L. 480 operations been negative, and we can conclude that P.L. 480 operations have helped to finance larger developments without larger budgetary deficit.

With regard to the impact of P.L. 480 operations on money supply, the monetary contraction (because of sales of food grains) has been nullified by a flow back into the economy via U.S. use expenditures, Cooley loans, and expenditure on developmental projects (including funds officially allocated and balances remaining to be invested in special securities). We came to the conclusion that P.L. 480 transactions have had a neutral effect on money supply.

To see the significance of P.L. 480 net support, we can look at the percentage of net support to the total budgetary receipts. Although the percentage has varied from year to year, the average support over the period as a whole has been 5.72% of the budget—a significant proportion. When P.L. 480 imports cease, net support will become negative. This means that 5.7% more budgetary receipts will have to be mobilized to have the same sized budget and enough funds will have to be mobilized to meet interest and principal payments on past P.L. 480 rupee loans.

TABLE 4.3. Net Support of P.L. 480 Aid to Government of India Budget

Indian Fiscal Years (Apr.–Mar.)	Loans to GOI	Grants to GOI	Investment in Special Securities	Total Receipts (1+2+3)	Loss on State Trading Account	Interest Payments by GOI	Loan Repayment by GOI	Transfer from SBI to RBI	Total Payments (5+6+7+8)	Net P.L. 480 Contribution	Total Budgetary Receipts
	1	2	3	4	5	6	7	8	9	10	11
					(Rs crores)						
1956–57	...	...	+ 32.95	+ 32.95	− 9.83	...	...	...	− 9.83	+ 23.12	865.08
1957–58	...	...	+ 107.20	+ 107.20	− 25.56	...	...	...	− 25.56	+ 91.74	971.00
1958–59	+ 5.00	...	+ 84.02	+ 89.02	− 6.23	...	...	...	− 6.23	+ 82.79	1,269.74
1959–60	+ 23.00	...	+ 62.59	+ 85.59	+ 10.77	...	...	...	+ 10.77	+ 96.36	1,536.51
1960–61	+ 49.90	+ 3.70	+ 215.37	+ 268.97	− 61.98	...	...	− 108.00	− 169.98	+ 98.99	2,004.46
1961–62	+ 54.00	+ 13.10	+ 36.78	+ 103.88	+ 9.40	− 0.20	...	− 36.00	− 27.01	+ 76.87	2,094.13
1962–63	+ 79.70	+ 54.00	+ 23.70	+ 157.40	− 22.17	− 3.83	− 0.01	− 50.00	− 76.01	+ 81.39	2,631.78
1963–64	+ 66.20	+ 63.50	+ 72.54	+ 202.24	− 32.02	− 6.15	− 0.06	− 30.00	− 68.23	+ 134.01	3,226.01
1964–65	+ 170.40	+ 122.00	− 21.10	+ 271.30	− 0.84	− 13.21	− 0.12	− 40.00	− 63.17	+ 208.13	3,725.63
1965–66	+ 80.00	+ 60.00	+ 112.00	+ 252.00	+ 27.74	− 17.08	− 0.29	− 21.00	− 10.63	+ 241.37	3,928.64
1966–67	+ 350.00	...	− 2.70	+ 347.30	+ 44.69	− 21.23	− 0.75	...	+ 22.71	+ 370.01	4,809.64
1967–68	+ 280.60	...	+ 93.60	+ 374.20	− 15.61[a]	− 26.26	− 1.31	...	− 43.18	+ 331.02	4,804.28
1968–69	+ 240.00	+ 8.50	− 59.60	+ 188.90	+ 154.76[b]	− 29.94	− 2.06	...	+ 122.52	+ 277.52	4,935.86
Total	+ 1,398.80	+ 324.80	+ 757.35	+ 2,480.95	+ 73.12	− 170.90	− 4.60	− 285.00	− 354.36	+ 2,103.22	367.95

Sources: (1) Figures in cols. 1, 2, and 3 are from *Economic Classification of the Budget*, Ministry of Finance, GOI. (2) Figures in cols. 6 and 7 are from Ministry of Finance. (3) Figures in col. 8 have been worked out on the basis of the agreed plan of the transfer of funds, *Reserve Bank of India Bulletin*, 1963.

a. Loss on figures has been worked out on the basis of estimated economic cost minus sale proceeds. This takes into account the changes in the stocks. See Appendix Table C-2 and C-3.

b. While budget papers do not show any surplus or deficit in realization of sale proceeds on P.L. 480 imports, present figure has been derived by taking into account estimated sale proceeds of imports under long-term dollar credit/sale basis.

Here we may point out a difference between the earlier aid repayable in rupees under P.L. 480 and the aid repayable in dollars. In the case of dollar aid, allocations for specified uses will be zero and funds will not be earmarked; yet GOI will get the funds from the sale proceeds of products imported under P.L. 480. In Table 4.3 these proceeds are reflected in the positive figure of Loss in State Trading Account (col. 5) in the last year. This means that as long as imports under P.L. 480 continue in any form, the net support may or may not become negative depending on the magnitude of lagged withdrawals of U.S. use and Cooley funds and on the fresh accruals in the form of receipts on the state trading account (L_i).

U.S. USE FUNDS. Commodity agreements between the recipient countries and the United States earmark a small portion of P.L. 480 counterpart funds for exclusive U.S. use. Besides this source of funds, the U.S. use funds (relating to P.L. 480) also accrue from loan repayment and interest payments by the recipient governments, loan repayment and interest payments by private firms under Cooley loans, and interest earned on the balances of U.S. Disbursing Office in the recipient countries. During past years the U.S. authorities were not free to use these funds at their discretion, since use of the funds was subject to approval by the U.S. Congress. If U.S. authorities in recipient countries wanted to use these funds over and above the amount approved by the Congress, they were to substitute them for dollar-funded projects. When the local currencies were overvalued in terms of exchange rates, U.S. authorities in recipient countries were not interested in substituting these funds for dollar-funded projects. Consequently balances have accumulated from past accruals (Table 4.4)—particularly large balances in India, Pakistan, United Arab Republic, Brazil, and Yugoslavia—and will continue to accrue around the turn of this century. This trend can be illustrated by an analysis of future accruals of these funds in India.

Accrual in India. At the end of fiscal year 1969 P.L. 480 rupee funds for U.S. use in India amounted to Rs 267 crores; if we include all rupee funds (P.L. 480 and other than P.L. 480 funds) the total was Rs 551 crores. Although the accrual of U.S. use funds from initial sales has come to an end since the cessation of imports themselves, the rupee funds will continue to mount because of reflows from the loan repayments and interest payments. U.S.-owned rupee funds are made up of five components: (1) principal repayments of Cooley loans, (2) interest payments on Cooley loans, (3) loan repayments by GOI,

TABLE 4.4. Title I, P.L. 480—Status of Foreign Currencies as of June 30, 1969 (million U.S. dollars).

| Country | Agreement Amounts through June 30, 1969 | Collections through June 30, 1969[a] | | Disbursements by Agencies through June 30, 1969[c,d] |
		Sale proceeds	Other proceeds[b]	
Afghanistan	1.0	1.0	...	1.5
Argentina	30.5	30.5	0.4	20.7
Australia	...	...	...	1.0
Austria	40.1	40.1	...	41.8
Belgium	...	...	...	6.0
Bolivia	37.1	36.9	2.3	33.8
Brazil	503.4	503.4	9.6	317.8
Burma	45.8	45.8	6.8	42.5
Canada	...	...	...	.7
Ceylon	31.5	31.5	2.2	27.4
Chile	85.2	85.2	9.0	70.4
China (Taiwan)	238.4	229.3	10.5	208.0
Colombia	66.2	66.2	12.5	61.4
Congo	85.0	85.0	.7	62.1
Costa Rica	...	...	...	.1
Cyprus	2.1	2.1	.1	2.4
Denmark	...	...	...	1.3
Dominican Republic	...	...	...	.7
Ecuador	11.5	11.5	1.4	12.2
El Salvador	...	...	...	(e)
Ethiopia	.8	.8	(e)	1.7
Finland	43.0	43.0	5.1	40.5
France	35.7	35.7	5.5	45.0
Germany	1.2	1.2	...	20.2
Ghana	36.5	23.7	.3	17.0
Greece	127.8	127.8	24.6	147.2
Guatemala	...	...	...	.3
Guinea	30.7	30.7	.5	4.7
Honduras	...	...	...	(e)
Hong Kong	...	...	...	4.0
Iceland	16.3	16.3	1.9	17.5
India	3,996.1	3,910.9	253.8	3,236.8
Indonesia	291.9	291.9	4.6	71.7
Iran	61.1	61.1	7.7	67.1
Ireland	...	...	...	.1
Israel	334.2	334.2	76.3	337.6
Italy	144.2	144.2	4.4	158.3
Ivory Coast	3.1	3.1	.1	2.8
Jamaica	...	...	...	.1
Japan	146.3	146.3	...	157.8
Jordan	5.9	5.9	.1	3.2
Kenya	...	...	...	.6
Korea	704.4	644.8	1.3	607.8
Lebanon	...	...	...	2.7
Liberia	...	...	...	(e)
Luxembourg	...	...	...	(e)
Malaysia	...	...	...	1.8

TABLE 4.4. *(continued)*

Country	Agreement Amounts through June 30, 1969	Collections through June 30, 1969[a]		Disbursements by Agencies through June 30, 1969[e,d]
		Sale proceeds	Other proceeds[b]	
Mali	.6	.6	. . .	.3
Mexico	25.2	25.2	5.8	31.7
Morocco	73.1	65.3	3.2	51.6
Nepal	. . .	. . .	.3	1.3
Netherlands	.3	.3	. . .	8.2
Nicaragua	. . .	. . .	. . .	(e)
Nigeria	. . .	. . .	. . .	1.1
Norway	. . .	. . .	. . .	1.0
Pakistan	1,248.3	1,237.6	68.8	1,188.0
Panama	. . .	. . .	. . .	.2
Paraguay	16.0	16.0	1.3	13.3
Peru	40.0	39.9	4.1	40.1
Philippines	53.2	53.2	3.3	53.7
Poland	519.5	519.5	. . .	44.9
Portugal	7.1	7.1	. . .	7.8
Senegal	3.3	3.3	. . .	2.7
Sierra Leone	. . .	. . .	. . .	.2
Singapore	. . .	. . .	. . .	(e)
South Africa	. . .	. . .	. . .	.7
Spain	488.0	488.0	29.1	428.5
Sudan	26.4	26.4	.2	18.4
Sweden	. . .	. . .	. . .	2.3
Switzerland	. . .	. . .	. . .	14.1
Syrian Arab Republic	34.9	34.9	1.2	25.4
Thailand	4.3	4.3	.3	10.8
Tunisia	91.1	85.3	4.5	72.0
Turkey	501.4	501.4	65.9	471.5
United Arab Republic (Cairo)	798.7	798.7	78.8	544.3
United Kingdom	48.5	48.5	. . .	57.6
Uruguay	36.2	36.2	2.8	21.1
Venezuela	. . .	. . .	. . .	1.2
Vietnam	615.4	557.8	.6	602.7
Yugoslavia	619.8	619.8	61.9	489.1
Total	12,408.3	12,159.4	773.8	10,064.1

Source: U.S. Congress, *Food for Peace,* p. 113.

a. Calculated at collection rates of exchange.

b. P.L. 480, sec. 104 (e) and (f) loan interest and repayment of principal and proceeds from sales of 104(g) commodities.

c. Prior to July 1961, disbursements under sec. 104(c), (g), and (f) grants were calculated at collection rates; sec. 104(a) sales at current Treasury selling rates; sec. 104(f) loans at loan agreement rates; sec. 104(b) (1), (e) loans, (b) (2) through (b) (5) at the weighted average rates at end of the month in which transfers were made to agency accounts for the balances remaining in the accounts. Subsequent to June 30, 1961, disbursements under sec. 104(a) through (j) are calculated at either the current Treasury selling rates or the end-of-the-quarter market rates.

d. Disbursements exceed collections in some countries because of conversions from other currencies.

e. Less than $50,000.

(4) interest payments by GOI, and (5) interest payments by the RBI on special securities. On the basis of existing agreements, reflows will continue to add to the U.S. accounts until the year 2010 (Table 4.5).

Projections of reflows in the U.S. accounts show that total U.S.-owned funds will grow at a compound rate of 19.6, 14.2, 12.4, and 6.6% during 1969–74, 1969–79, 1969–84, and 1969–2010 (Table 4.6). As loans are repaid, the rate of growth continues to fall and will become negligible (an interest of 1.5% will continue to accrue after every other source goes dry) after the year 2010. Even if we take the rate of increase over the period as a whole (6.6%), it is fairly rapid considering the large base (Rs 551 crores at the end of fiscal year 1969).

The average contribution of loan repayment and interest payments by GOI to the U.S.-owned funds works out to be around 70% over the period as a whole (Table 4.7). Then comes the loan repayment and interest payment by the private firms under Cooley loans. If we assume that nothing is withdrawn from these balances, the average contribution of interest on special securities to total increase in the U.S. use funds continues to decline because the contribution of other components increases (loan repayment installments increase in geometrical progression). However, for the period as a whole the contribution of this source would be as high as 25% of the increase in total U.S.-owned P.L. 480 counterpart funds despite a rate of interest as low as 1.5%.

The significance of these accumulating U.S.-owned funds can be highlighted by looking into the proportions of these funds to the projected total money supply in the economy. To do so will require projections of the money supply itself. In India a number of models (both single equation and simultaneous equation) have been tried in order to estimate the money demand functions. These models were surveyed recently by Khusro.[9] National income has been one of the most significant explanatory variables common to all models. Since the projections of national income are available with some degree of certainty, we have used national income as the only explanatory variable in money demand function, and we have added the intercept term to pick up the effect of the rest of the explanatory variables. This may be a crude method but is sufficient for our limited purpose: to visualize the potential significance of U.S.-owned rupee funds for monetary management in the country. The estimated equation $D = a + bY$ is as follows:

$$D = 9.98 + 0.2050Y \qquad R^2 = 0.97$$
$$(0.0521)$$

TABLE 4.5. Long-Term Projections of U.S. Use Rupee Funds in India (Rs crores)

U.S. Fiscal Years (July 1– June 30)	Principal Repayment, Cooley Loans	Interest Payment, Cooley Loans	Principal Repayment, 104 (f)	Interest Payment, 104 (f)	Interest by RBI on Special Securities	Total P.L. 480 (1+2+3+4+5)	Non-P.L. 480 Loan Repayment and Interest Payment	Interest on Non-P.L. 480 by RBI	Total (7+8)	Grand Total (6+9)
	1	2	3	4	5	6	7	8	9	10
1969	11.92	13.71	5.38	125.43	33.85	190.29	229.63	54.09	283.72	474.01
1970	17.04	17.94	8.66	158.50	37.39	239.53	269.35	58.94	328.29	567.82
1971	23.32	22.21	13.06	192.65	41.67	292.91	308.61	64.39	373.00	665.91
1972	30.46	26.62	18.59	226.64	46.74	349.05	345.72	70.41	416.13	761.85
1973	36.96	31.32	25.26	260.44	52.59	406.57	381.04	76.96	458.00	954.57
1974	45.60	35.60	33.09	294.01	59.27	467.57	415.15	84.03	499.18	966.75
1975	58.41	39.34	42.08	327.31	66.77	528.91	446.76	91.59	538.35	1,067.26
1976	60.88	42.48	52.25	360.31	75.09	591.01	475.98	99.59	575.57	1,166.58
1977	68.66	45.03	63.76	392.98	84.24	654.67	500.02	107.96	607.98	1,262.65
1978	75.41	47.01	80.61	425.73	94.27	723.03	522.33	116.67	638.69	1,361.72
1979	81.43	48.48	102.94	459.94	105.28	798.07	541.47	125.67	667.14	1,465.21
1980	85.94	49.52	127.77	493.54	117.26	874.03	557.87	134.92	692.79	1,566.82
1981	89.22	50.23	155.15	526.86	130.23	959.69	573.74	144.41	718.15	1,677.84
1982	92.11	50.69	184.62	559.38	144.19	1,030.99	586.10	154.06	740.16	1,771.15
1983	95.00	50.92	216.20	591.09	159.16	1,112.37	595.74	163.69	759.43	1,871.80
1984	95.60	50.97	249.91	621.93	175.13	1,193.54	603.40	173.64	777.04	1,970.58
1985	95.90	50.98	285.78	651.83	193.88	1,278.37	611.14	183.70	794.84	2,073.21
1986			323.82	680.73	209.87	1,361.30	618.95	193.88	812.83	2,174.13
1987			364.07	708.59	228.90	1,448.44	626.85	204.14	830.99	2,279.43
1988			406.54	735.35	248.98	1,537.75	634.83	214.56	849.39	2,387.14
1989			451.27	760.95	270.13	1,629.23	642.87	225.11	867.98	2,497.21
1990			498.27	785.34	292.37	1,722.86	651.00	235.78	886.78	2,609.64
1991			547.58	808.45	315.71	1,818.62	659.19	246.58	906.07	2,725.29
1992			599.22	830.24	340.17	1,916.51	667.46	257.50	924.96	2,841.47
1993			653.22	850.66	365.76	2,016.52	675.81	268.55	944.36	2,960.88

TABLE 4.5. (*continued*)

U.S. Fiscal Years (July 1– June 30)	Principal Repayment, Cooley Loans	Interest Payment, Cooley Loans	Principal Repayment, 104 (f)	Interest Payment, 104 (f)	Interest by RBI on Special Securities	Total P.L. 480 (1+2+3 +4+5)	Non-P.L. 480 Loan Repayment and Interest Payment	Interest on Non-P.L. 480 by RBI	Total (7+8)	Grand Total (6+9)
	1	2	3	4	5	6	7	8	9	10
1994			709.61	869.60	392.50	2,118.59	684.22	279.73	963.95	3,082.54
1995			787.42	887.02	420.69	2,244.01	692.71	291.03	983.74	3,227.75
1996			829.68	902.86	449.77	2,329.19	698.49	302.43	1,000.92	3,330.11
1997			893.45	917.05	480.03	2,437.41	704.06	313.92	1,017.98	3,455.39
1998			959.70	929.53	511.49	2,547.60	708.34	325.47	1,033.81	3,581.41
1999			1,028.52	940.23	544.16	2,659.79				3,693.60
2000			1,094.28	949.14	577.97	2,768.27				3,802.08
2001			1,156.07	956.41	612.83	2,872.19				3,906.00
2002			1,211.21	962.31	648.92	2,969.32				4,003.13
2003			1,265.86	967.02	685.62	3,065.38				4,099.19
2004			1,319.79	970.62	723.20	3,160.49				4,194.30
2005			1,368.48	973.19	761.20	3,102.87				4,136.63
2006			1,412.03	974.97	800.61	3,334.49				4,368.30
2007			1,452.74	976.05	840.28	3,415.95				4,449.76
2008			1,469.71	976.52	880.24	3,473.35				4,507.16
2009			1,472.00	976.64	920.24	3,515.76				4,549.57
2010			1,474.36	976.69	960.27	3,558.20				4,592.01

Source: Projected Repayment Schedule of P.L. 480 Funds, Program Division, USAID, India, 1968.
Note: The cumulative figure of interest paid by RBI on accumulated funds at the end of fiscal 1969 has been divided between P.L. 480 and non–P.L. 480 on the basis of proportion of these cumulative funds. Separate figures on these are not available. Subsequently the rate of interest of 1½% has been applied on accumulated funds.

TABLE 4.6. Rate of Growth of P.L. 480 Funds in India on Basis of Existing Agreements to End of Fiscal 1969 (percent)

Variables	Rate of Increase[a]			
	1969–74	1969–79	1969–84	1969–2010
1. Principal repayments of Cooley loans	30.4	20.5	13.9	2.9
2. Interest payments on Cooley loans	20.4	13.0	8.1	1.6
3. Loan repayment by GOI (104 f)	43.5	32.6	27.7	13.1
4. Interest payments by GOI (104 f)	18.4	13.3	10.5	4.2
5. Interest on P.L. 480 deposits	11.9	12.2	11.8	8.5
Total U.S. Use Funds	19.6	14.2	12.4	6.6

Source: Calculated from data in Table 4.5.

a. These are worked out by fitting the function $Y = ab^t$, where t is the time (independent variable) and Y is the series of each component separately.

where

$$D = \text{money demand (both currency and demand deposits)}$$

$$Y = \text{national income at current prices in crores of rupees}$$

Since on an ex post basis demand for money and money supply are equal, we have used money supply data (1950–51 to 1967–68) to estimate the money demand function. The equation means that for every increase in national income of 1 crore rupees, money demand will increase by 0.2 crore rupees or approximately 20%. If we further assume that money demand is met by a corresponding monetary increase, we can project future money supply based on the projections of national income.

We made three projections of money supply corresponding to three projections of national income (at current prices). The three projections of national income are (1) a 4% increase (implying a slight decline in prices, if output grows by 6%), (2) a 6% increase (the plan target and with no increase in prices), and (3) an 8% increase (which implies an increase in prices). These three estimates are termed low, medium, and high estimates of income, and we worked out three corresponding estimates of money supply. We used these three estimates

TABLE 4.7. Average Contribution of Various Components to U.S. Rupee Funds on Basis of Agreements to End of Fiscal 1969 (percent)

Variables	1969–74	1969–79	1969–84	1969–2010
1. Principal repayments of Cooley loans	12.1	12.0	9.0	1.6
2. Interest payments on Cooley loans	7.9	5.9	3.7	0.5
3. Loan repayments by GOI (104 f)	10.0	15.5	23.9	48.0
4. Interest payments by GOI (104 f)	60.8	55.6	49.3	24.3
5. Interest on P.L. 480 deposits	9.2	10.9	14.1	25.8
Total U.S. Use Funds	100	100	100	100

Sources: Calculations based on data in Table 4.5.

of money supply to determine the proportion of total money supply that surplus U.S.-owned rupee funds in India will make up. We determined the magnitude of surplus U.S. use funds by deducting the expected withdrawals by the U.S. Embassy in India. There is no exact estimate of U.S. needs for rupee funds in the near future. In February 1970 U.S. Embassy officials estimated Rs 400 million per annum; USAID officials put the estimate at Rs 445.4 million or Rs 44.54 crores, which is the level actually obtained of the fiscal year 1969 (see appendix Table C-4).[10] We have set the expected withdrawals for U.S. uses at the higher of these two estimates—i.e., Rs 44.54 crores per annum. We could find a reasonable basis for the projections of national income only up to 1983–84, so we confined our illustration of the potential magnitude of surplus funds up to 1983–84 (but surplus funds would continue to accrue long after this date).

The proportion of surplus (as defined earlier) U.S.-owned P.L. 480 funds ranges between 3.11% and 5.68% of money supply respectively under high and low assumptions about the increase in money supply (Table 4.8). If we consider the proportion of total U.S.-owned rupee funds in India to the projected money supply, the proportion ranges between 7.45% and 13.62% until the end of 1984.

Utilization. The problem of accumulating surplus U.S.-owned local currency funds is not confined to India; it is common to all the major recipient countries. The U.S. authorities are faced with a long-term problem of using these counterpart funds without causing additional inflationary pressure in the recipient countries—a problem further complicated because the real aid flow has stopped in some countries. The use of these funds would require a net outgo from the budgetary resources depending on the type of use of these surplus funds. This problem can be illustrated by analyzing the Indian situation again.

These surplus funds can be officially allocated for Indian use within the framework of the existing plan or be used by enlarging the plan, so they will either be neutral to plan expenditures (and neutral to money supply) or be an addition to the existing plan expenditure (and expansionary in impact for money supply).

MONDALE AMENDMENT. Before the addition of the Mondale amendment to section 104 of P.L. 480, U.S.-owned local currency funds could be used only for U.S. purposes and third-country assistance purposes listed in subsections (a) to (j), as discussed in Chapter 1. Even under these legal provisions U.S. authorities in India were not

TABLE 4.8. Projected Surplus U.S. Use Rupee Funds of **Low, Medium, and High Estimates of Money Supply** (percent).

		Years												
U.S. Use Rupee Funds	1968–69			1973–74			1978–79			1983–84		
	Low	Medium	High	Low	Medium	High	Low	Medium	High	Low	Medium	High
Surplus P.L. 480 funds	4.37	4.45	4.53	3.58	4.01	4.49	3.19	3.91	4.83	3.11	4.19	5.68
Total surplus Rupee funds	9.01	9.18	9.35	9.13	10.22	11.45	8.31	10.21	12.58	7.45	10.05	13.62

free to use surplus P.L. 480 funds at their discretion. All uses pursuant to sections 104 (a) and (b) were subject to the appropriation processes of the U.S. Congress. If U.S. authorities in India wanted to increase their expenditures, they were required to increase their dollar appropriations, to ask for a special foreign currency appropriation, or to otherwise substitute their dollar-funded projects with rupee holdings. Consequently, despite the fact that surplus P.L. 480 rupees were available, they could not be used in unlimited quantities.

The Mondale amendment provides for certain exceptions to the norm concerning the countries considered excess-currency countries. Under this amendment, excess funds can be used for two types of purposes: (1) acquisition of sites (building and grounds) by the United States and (2) assistance to the recipient country in undertaking measures of self-help to increase its production of agricultural commodities and its facilities for the storage and distribution of such commodities. These exceptions differ in their economic effect: the first would add to aggregate current consumption expenditure of GOI; the second could remain neutral or expansionary to budgetary expenditure depending on whether the allocations were for projects already included in the plan or for projects added to the plan. We have taken into account expenditures under the first exception while working out surplus rupee funds. Further discussion will explore the consequences of allocation of surplus funds for Indian use.

PLAN PROJECTS. The Mondale amendment provides for the allocation of surplus funds in excess-currency countries for projects that promote agricultural development and other measures of self-help. The five-year plans being implemented in India provide a project mix that contains all of these kinds of projects. One way to use surplus funds would be to give assistance for some of the projects listed in the plan. In this event (we will recall from the analysis in the previous section) there would be no effect on monetary flows. This can be illustrated as follows:

GOI BUDGET

Incomings	Rs	Outgoings	Rs
Grants from U.S. Embassy	+100	Investment in special securities	—100

The grants of U.S.-owned rupee funds would be just equal to the funds required for redeeming the special securities. There would be no expansion or reduction in the money supply and no budgetary deficit or surplus; the projects tied to these funds would be financed as they have been financed earlier. In this case, since the project would already be a part of the budget, tying it to P.L. 480 funds would not necessitate any additional expenditure in the economy that was not taken into account in the plan.

This procedure makes the official allocations of surplus funds neutral to the plan and amounts to a permanent freezing of the funds. Since there is no economic effect, surplus P.L. 480 funds can be given to GOI in any manner—either as a fixed amount or at some rate synchronized with the accrual of these funds.

ADDITIONAL PROJECTS. If the surplus funds were to be used for purposes other than plan projects, their use would generate additional monetary flows into the economy via GOI budgetary deficits or enlargement of budgetary deficits if the budget is already in deficit. In this case expenditures on projects would be over and above what was already planned, and the situation would be as follows:

GOI BUDGET

Incomings	Rs	Outgoings	Rs
Grants from U.S. Embassy	+100	Investment in special securities	—100
		Expenditures of contracted additional projects	—100

If funds worth Rs 100 were given to the GOI for additional projects, they would involve an addition to the GOI expenditure worth the same amount. The impact of this investment on the incomes and additional demands can be visualized in the simple Keynesian model. In this framework the investment multiplier K is defined as $1/s + g + m$, where s, g, and m represent marginal savings, taxation, and import rates. In the Indian situation we found the values to be 9%, 9%, and 8% for s, g, and m respectively.[11]

On this basis the Keynesian investment-income multiplier works out to be 3.85. An analysis of the pattern of consumption expenditures on food grains based on various rounds of the National Sample Survey suggests that the expenditure (value of purchased) elasticity for cereals in value terms is in the range of 0.5–0.6. The corresponding quantity elasticities range between 0.35 and 0.45. The elasticity for pulses was observed to be in the range of 0.6–0.7 in terms of quantity and 0.7–0.9 in terms of value.[12] If we assume the coefficient for income elasticity of demand to be 0.5 or 0.6, 50–60% of increased income will go to the purchase of food, so the first thing to look for is the supply of food grains from domestic sources.

Projections of food grain supply and demand. The food grain output in India increased at a very slow compound rate of 3% from 1949–50 to 1964–65. On the basis of extrapolation from this past trend, recent increases in food grain production do not appear to be very spectacular. A GOI study noted:

It would be helpful to recall that the food grain output for each of the years 1967–68 to 1969–70 has been below the corresponding values extrapolated for the years on the basis of the trend line for the preceding period, 1949–50 to 1964–65, representing a compound rate of 3 percent per annum. In fact even the bumper output realized in 1970–71 exceeds only moderately the value extrapolated for this year. There seems little basis here for the inference that food grain output of the country in recent years has moved away to a higher growth path. Perhaps the inference rests on the belief that the recent upward drift in food output, since initiated by the new force of modern technology, should be treated as a new trend destined to continue in the future.[13]

A few recent studies show that modern technology has at last begun to play its role in production of the agricultural sector, and the views expressed in the GOI report may not be a realistic description of the future trend in food grain production.[14] We have to account for the increased role of modern inputs which have been responsible for recent increases in agricultural production. A study by the National Council of Applied Economic Research (NCAER) projected food grain production on the basis of projected availability of modern inputs and gross area under each crop in India.[15] This study also projected demand for food grains up to 1985–86. Corresponding to two sets of demand estimates (high and low), two sets of supply-demand estimates are presented in Table 4.9, which show that there would be a surplus of food grains starting from 1970–71. The magnitude of surplus will range between 1.81 and 2.52 million tons in 1975–76, 5.49 and 7.05 million tons in 1980–81, and 7.22 and 9.69 million tons in 1985–86. These figures show that India would soon be in a position to generate a domestic

TABLE 4.9. Projections of Import Demand (−) for or Export Surplus (+) of Food Grains in India

1970–71

Commodity	Expected supply for human consumption[a]	Projected aggregate demand		Balance (supply to demand)	
		high	low	high	low
		(million tons)			
Rice	39.06	37.78	37.62	+1.28	+1.44
Wheat	19.67	20.07	20.00	−0.40	−0.33
All cereals	81.50	80.67	80.59	+0.83	+0.91
Pulses	10.50	10.55	10.48	−0.05	+0.02
Food grains	92.00	91.24	91.04	+0.76	+0.96
		1980–81			
Rice	49.29	48.29	47.19	+1.00	2.10
Wheat	30.40	29.19	27.91	+1.21	+2.49
All cereals	107.17	102.38	102.07	+4.79	+5.10
Pulses	15.75	14.41	13.97	+1.34	+1.78
Food grains	122.92	117.43	115.87	+5.49	+7.05

1975–76

Commodity	Expected supply for human consumption[a]	Projected aggregate demand		Balance (supply to demand)	
		high	low	high	low
		(million tons)			
Rice	43.71	42.65	42.09	+1.06	+1.62
Wheat	25.03	24.27	23.68	+0.76	+1.35
All cereals	93.08	90.88	90.82	+2.20	+2.26
Pulses	12.25	12.32	12.11	−0.07	+0.14
Food grains	105.33	103.52	102.81	+1.81	+2.52
		1985–86			
Rice	58.97	55.90	54.09	+3.07	+4.88
Wheat	36.65	36.20	33.95	+0.45	+2.70
All cereals	125.25	118.08	117.68	+7.17	+7.57
Pulses	18.38	17.25	16.60	+1.13	+1.78
Food grains	143.63	136.41	133.94	+7.22	+9.69

Source: National Council of Applied Economic Research (in cooperation with the Center for Agricultural and Rural Development, I.S.U.), *Demand and Supply Projections of Food Grains For India 1970–71 to 1985–86*, pp. 37, 38.

a. The requirements for seed, feed, and wastage (as a percentage to total production) are: rice 7.00, wheat 10.60, other cereals 21.56, and total pulses 12.50.

TABLE 4.10. Projected Food Grain Demand and Supply, All India

	1968–69	1973–74	1978–79	1983–84
		(million tons)		
Demand for all food grains	106.46	129.27	158.99	198.62
for human consumption	89.43	108.59	133.55	166.84
for seed, feed, and wastage	17.03	20.68	25.44	31.78
Production of food grains	94.01	129.27	158.99	198.62

Source: S. K. Ray, "Food Grain Demand and Supply—Projections of Regional Imbalances," pp. A59–74.

food grain surplus. However, NCAER estimates of surplus food grains are on the high side because of a low figure of income elasticity of demand: the income elasticity of demand for food grains ranges between 0.13 (low) and 0.23 (high).[16]

    S. K. Ray recently made an alternative projection of food grain supply and demand on the basis of exhaustive micro level estimates of food grain production crop by crop and state by state.[17] Ray's projections of food grain supply are also based on a projected availability of modern inputs and land area. The projections of food grain demand (at the aggregate level) were calculated by working out the projections of per capita demand in rural and urban sectors and multiplying them by the population estimates. The income elasticity coefficient for all India has been estimated at 0.55. The values of rural and urban income elasticity coefficients are 0.60 and 0.30 respectively.[18] On the basis of these coefficients and of projected national income figures (4.0, 5.5, and 6.0% respectively [compound rates] during fourth, fifth, and sixth five-year plans), food grain demand has been projected up to the year 1983–84 (Table 4.10). These food grain supply (normal weather) and demand estimates show that despite the technological breakthrough and associated upward shifts in production functions, there is little evidence of the availability of any sizable surplus of food grains from domestic sources which can be used to match the additional demand for food grains created by expenditures from the U.S.-owned surplus rupee funds. If there are small surpluses, they would be necessary for the buffer stock operations to mitigate year-to-year fluctuations in output due to weather conditions.

MINIMUM MULTIPLIER EFFECT. If additional projects are to be set up with surplus U.S.-owned rupee funds, the resulting multiplier effect could be minimized by making additional grants of food grains (under Title II). Let us assume that a project of Rs 100 crores investment is started and out of it Rs 70 crores go directly for wage payments,

Rs 20 crores go for purchase of other domestic services and materials, and Rs 10 crores go for purchase of equipment from abroad. According to the example presented in Chapter 1, if the food demand arising out of the investment is met by aid, the multiplier effect itself is dampened (1.4850 instead of 3.85 before), mainly because domestic producers do not increase their income out of additional demand for food during various rounds. The total impact of Rs 100 crores of investment will exhaust itself in 10 rounds of expenditure. In India, to assume an income-expenditure lag of three months or four rounds of expenditure is considered reasonable.[19] On this basis it will take two and a half years to exhaust the impact of Rs 100 crores of additional investment, which will generate an additional food demand of Rs 60.43 crores in money terms.

A weighted average of various food grain prices in India shows that Rs 105 crores are equivalent to 1 million tons of food grains at 1970–71 prices. On this basis, additional demand of Rs 60.43 crores is equivalent to 0.561 million tons in quantity terms. If the surplus (total) accumulation of U.S.-owned funds in India up to 1986 (Rs 1970.58 — Rs 668.10 crores for U.S. expenditure) is to be used, additional food demand generated out of this investment would be about 7.3 million tons spread over the next 17-year period up to 1986. If this magnitude of total food aid is provided under Title II during the next 17 years (which amounts to an average of less than half a million tons of food every year), surplus funds can be used for creating additional projects. But this will also cause an increase in demand for materials and foreign exchange, which will have to be met by diverting these resources from their planned use.

CHAPTER FIVE

Food Aid for Economic Development

THE OUTLOOK for food as a tool for economic development has undergone a considerable change during the last few years. Rapid increases in food grain production have resulted in a grain balance at existing levels of economic development in some of the larger recipient countries in Asia. At the same time there has been considerably less economic pressure in the United States for the disposal of surplus agricultural commodities. This state of affairs has led to increasing economic and political pressure for hardening of the terms of food aid and changed the nature of food aid itself. Therefore, an assessment of potentials and prospects of using food aid for additional economic development must be made by taking account of likely trends of the changes already under way both in the United States and in recipient countries.

POTENTIALS. The technological transformation known as the Green Revolution has been under way in Asia in recent years, characterized by biological-mechanical innovations that have rapidly increased output and total net revenue of the agricultural sector.[1] Figure 5.1 shows total cost (TC), total revenue (TR), and total output with old and new techniques for agriculture taken as a single industry. The curve TR represents total revenue, C_1 represents the cost before the innovation, and C_2 represents the cost after the innovation. Per unit costs are lower with C_2 than C_1, as shown by the lesser slope of OC compared to OA. We assume that normative profit maximization motive prevails; hence at the equilibrium for industry, total cost, total revenue, and total output are U_1A, U_1B and OU_1 respectively before the innovation. Total revenue increases, but the total cost decreases at the equilibrium under the new technique (C_2); new profit (CD) is much larger than profit under the old technique (AB), and the agricultural sector increases its output and improves its income because of the new technology.

The distribution of the total gain to the agricultural sector among various factors, various farm sizes, and various groups dependent on agriculture for their livelihood has been subject to considerable de-

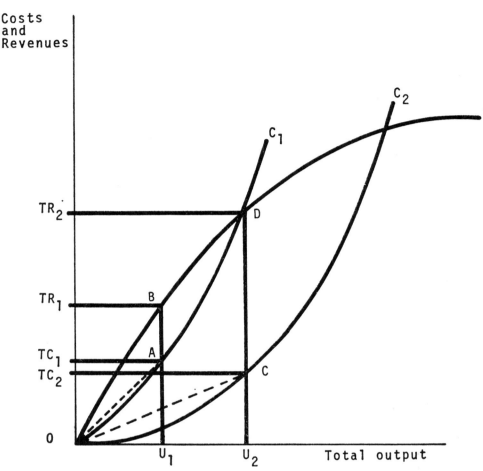

Fig. 5.1. *Change in net revenue (TR — TC) with technological change.*

bate.[2] Factor shares are mainly a function of the elasticity of product demand, the elasticity of factor substitution, and the "biassedness" of technological change introduced by expanding use of some factors during the Green Revolution. Government policies in most of the developing countries have been committed to the maintenance of minimum support prices for major agricultural commodities, and the elasticity of product demand as such becomes irrelevant: the absolute shares of all the factors will increase with the increase in output. Recent studies confirm this increase.[3] But the relative shares have not increased proportionately. Empirical results show that technological change in these countries has labor-saving bias. Agricultural laborers' incomes rise less than farmers' incomes with the increase in crop production.[4] Interfarm income disparity has also increased because of high rate of adoption of new technology by the larger farms compared with smaller farms.[5]

Despite increased incomes of the agricultural sector, rural poverty and unemployment have become a growing concern. In India, for example, recent studies show that a large proportion of rural population have incomes below the abject poverty line. Minhas recently worked out the percentage of people below minimum level of living in rural India.[6] His calculations show some decline in the percentage of people below the poverty line in the last few years, yet 50.6% of the people were below the poverty line in 1967–68 on the basis of Rs 240 per annum as the definition of poverty line (Table 5.1). This percentage is lower (37.1%) on the basis of an alternative definition of poverty line (Rs 200 per annum). Bardhan's calculations, on the other hand, show an increase in percentage of people below the poverty line from 38.0 in 1960–61 to 63.1 in 1967–68[7] (Table 5.2). The exact percentage is a matter of academic interest, but the fact is that large numbers of the rural population do not have enough income to buy the quantities of food required for good nutrition.

Two alternatives are open to these low-income countries: (1) massive food distribution programs and/or (2) increasing employment and thereby increasing incomes of the poor. Lele argues, "The alternative of massive food distribution is politically unfeasible in low-income countries unless food production provides at least marginal surpluses at an aggregate level or unless the countries are centrally controlled."[8] Recent studies show that despite the Green Revolution, the projected availability of calories and proteins is not likely to exceed the minimum nutritional target. For example, in India the projection reveals that the

TABLE 5.1. Percentage and Number of People below Minimum Level of Living: Rural India

Year	Below Rs 240 per Annum		Below Rs 200 per Annum	
	%	millions	%	millions
1956–57	65.0	215	52.4	173
1957–58	63.2	212	50.2	169
1960–61	59.4	211	46.0	164
1961–62	56.4	206	43.6	159
1963–64	57.8	221	44.2	169
1964–65	51.6	202	39.3	154
1967–68	50.6	210	37.1	154

Source: B. S. Minhas, "Rural Poverty, Land Redistribution, and Development Strategy," p. 102.

TABLE 5.2.   Percentage of Rural People below Rs 15 per Month at 1960–61 Prices

	1960–61	1964–65	1967–68
1. Consumer price index	100.0	144.0	199.5
2. Current value of goods worth Rs 15 at 1960–61 prices (Rs)	15.0	21.6(21)	29.9(28)
3. Percentage of rural people (approx.) below Rs 15 per month at 1960–61 prices:			
(a) Unadjusted	38.0	44.6+	73.2+
(b) Adjusted	38.0	31.8+	63.1+

Source: Pranab K. Bardhan, "On the Minimum Levels of Living and the Rural Poor," p. 130.

Note: For consumer price indices for each July–June agricultural year we have taken the simple average of the Labour Bureau indices for two calendar years. The index for 1964–65 is, however, an average of 12 months from September 1964 to August 1965, since July and August 1964 figures are not available. The bracketed numbers in row 2 are the conservative approximations we have used for our analysis. The estimates in row 3 are based on National Sample Survey data on percentage distribution of persons by rural per capita expenditure groups at current prices for Rounds 16, 19, and 22. The method of adjustment used for the estimates in row 3(b) is explained in the text. The + signs in rows 3(a) and 3(b) indicate that the actual percentages are somewhat above the figures mentioned.

minimum nutritional target for both calories and proteins is not going to be exceeded even by 1981 (Table 5.3). With this aggregate picture, we can see that massive food distribution programs cannot be sustained from domestic sources.

Another alternative is to create more employment and thereby additional effective demand for food. We discussed this idea (Chapter 1) that food aid can be absorbed for additional development programs even though domestic supply is enough to take care of effective demand at the existing level of development programs. The problem of employment generation in the agricultural sector in low-income countries is all the

TABLE 5.3.   Availability of Calories and Proteins

	Base Level 1969	Projected 1981	Minimum Nutritional Target by Sukhatme
Total calories (rounded)	1,965	2,300	2,370
Vegetable proteins (gm)	45.5	54.4	55.6
Animal proteins (gm)	5.2	6.3	10.0
Total proteins (gm)	50.7	60.7	65.6
Percentage of animal protein to total protein	10.3	10.3	15.2

Source: J. S. Sharma, "Feeding India's Population in 1980—A Quantitative Assessment."

TABLE 5.4. Extrapolation beyond 1985 of Projections of Asian Population for 1962–85 (in millions)

Year	Total Population (+ 2.5% per annum)	Nonagricultural Population (+ 3.8% per annum)	Agricultural Population	Agricultural as Percentage of Total
1962	833	250	583	70
1985	1,471	591	880	60
2000	2,130	1,030	1,100	52
2020	3,490	2,180	1,310	38
2030	4,470	3,170	1,300	29
2040	5,720	4,600	1,120	20
2050	7,320	6,670	650	9

Source: FAO/UN, *Provisional Indicative World Plan for Agricultural Development*, p. 16.

more important because of a low rate of increase in off-farm employment. The cost of job creation in the nonagricultural sector is high. Consequently, "nearly half of the additional people between 1962–1985 would need to be absorbed in the agricultural sector."[9] The situation is not likely to improve even up to the end of this century (Table 5.4).

The use of food aid for employment-generating projects requires extreme caution lest it dampen the incentives of domestic producers, particularly when the farmers are in the process of adopting modern inputs. Our analysis in Chapter 2 shows that it can be achieved by creating a differentiated market for food aid commodities. The method of distribution determines which group will or will not participate directly in food aid programs. Group differentiation provides the key for capitalizing on certain characteristics of consumer behavior and allows for stressing those characteristics that will promote effective use of food aid to achieve specified objectives. Besides the differentiated market for imported commodities, minimum support prices will have to be more effectively enforced if the negative price, production, and income impacts of food aid are to be minimized.

Changing the Commodity Mix. Cereals provide more than half of the total proteins in human diets in the developing countries except in Latin America. As money incomes increase, the demand for livestock products increases rapidly. An idea of projected demand and supply of livestock products in developing countries is shown in Table 5.5. An FAO study noted that poultry and pork are the two branches of the livestock industry that promise a faster turnover both biologically and technically.[10] The study also notes:

TABLE 5.5. Growth Rates Proposed for Livestock Production and Comparisons with Demand[a] **(percent per annum 1962–85)**

Region	Meat Production[b] as per reg. studies	Meat incl. addit. pork and poultry	Meat Demand	Milk Prod.	Milk Demand	Eggs Prod.	Eggs Demand	Imbalance Meat[b] as per reg. studies	Imbalance Meat incl. addit. pork and poultry	Imbalance Milk	Imbalance Eggs
Africa south of the Sahara	3.4	4.4	4.4	2.4	3.5	4.9	4.6	1,055	1	762	−171
Asia and Far East	3.5	5.6	5.6	2.8	5.4	5.9	6.4	3,288	−2	26,294	−109
River Plate Countries[d]	2.6	2.6	1.5	2.3	1.7	2.6	2.4	−2,980[e]	−2,980[e]	−3,609	−236
Rest of Latin America	3.3	4.1	4.3	3.4	4.3	4.5	4.5	2,213	156	4,848	−70
Near East and N.W. Africa	3.1	4.1	4.4	2.6	4.0	4.4	4.8	1,460	553	5,761	−9
Total	3.2	4.1	4.2	2.9	4.6	4.8	4.9	5,036	−2,272	34,056	−595

(The column group "Annual Imbalance by 1985 between Food Demand and Production Objectives[c] (000 metric tons)" spans the last four columns.)

Source: FAO/UN, *Provisional Indicative World Plan for Agricultural Development*, p. 36.

a. Growth rates refer to output and exclude inventories.

b. The first column shows the outcome of the regional studies; the second is based on the higher pig and poultry growth proposed in the world study.

c. The minus sign denotes a surplus. In the case of eggs the surplus is an "apparent" one arising from the use of "food demand" on the demand side while the production objectives were set to account for food demand plus hatching eggs and wastage. These factors added 10–15% to food demand for the whole of the "apparent" surplus.

d. Argentina, Uruguay, and Paraguay.

e. The export availability would be less than this since the figure shown here includes edible offals, much of which is probably not exportable.

Success would be, however, conditional on a number of factors. First, a heavy input of concentrate feeds will be essential, and at prices more favorable to the livestock sector than has traditionally been the case in the developing countries. *110 million tons of concentrate would be required for the livestock sector as a whole by 1985 compared to 83 million tons in the regional studies and only 31 million tons in 1962.* Not only will there have to be a satisfactory feed grain: product price, but a reasonable assurance of an even flow of grain.[11]

In the circumstances of marginal surplus and presence of weather cycles, such an assurance is hard to find from the domestic supply sources.

During previous decades low-income countries have used food aid mainly for direct human consumption. If the product mix of food aid is changed to include more feed grains, it can be used to increase the production of the livestock industry in recipient countries without causing any price decline for domestic producers. Israel provides an example of such a transformation of food aid commodities to increase livestock production. Price decline for domestic producers can be prevented by distributing the imported feed grains through a special market channel.

Developing New Export Outlets. Food aid in the form of feed grains can help develop new export outlets in developing countries, and such aid may be made self-supporting. Exports of meat, particularly beef and veal, are a case in point. There is a strong demand for meat on the international market. An FAO/UN study noted that South American countries are particularly well placed to develop their meat production and exports.[12] Central American, East African, and Asian countries may also be able to take advantage of export demand for meat. However, the availability of food aid alone will not help create a new export outlet for meat because of foot-and-mouth disease in most of these countries, particularly South American countries. The control of this disease must be undertaken as a first priority.

PROSPECTS. The idea of food aid originated from mutual interests of the United States and recipient countries. The prospects of food aid during the next decade or two will again depend on the mutual interests of the United States and recipient countries in the changed agricultural situation.

Donor's Point of View. The pressure of accumulating surplus stocks with CCC was the main motivating force behind food aid in the 1950s. Since then the production control measures have

TABLE 5.6.   Carryover of Major Farm Commodities in the United States, 1950–71

Year[a]	Wheat	Cotton	Food Grains
	(million bushels)	(million bales)	(million tons)
1950	424.7	6.8	30.5
1951	399.9	2.3	28.6
1952	256.0	2.8	20.1
1953	605.5	5.6	27.0
1954	933.5	9.7	31.7
1955	1,036.2	11.2	39.1
1956	1,033.5	14.5	43.2
1957	908.8	11.3	48.8
1958	881.4	8.7	59.0
1959	1,295.1	8.9	67.5
1960	1,313.5	7.6	74.6
1961	1,411.2	7.2	85.0
1962	1,321.9	7.8	72.2
1963	1,194.9	11.2	64.4
1964	901.2	12.4	69.3
1965	817.3	14.3	54.8
1966	535.2	16.9	42.1
1967	425.0	12.5	37.1
1968	539.4	6.4	48.3
1969	818.6	6.5	50.2
1970	884.2	5.7	48.4
1971	730.2[b]	4.5[b]	35.0[b]

Source: USDA, *1971 Handbook of Agricultural Charts,* Agr. Handbook 443 (Washington: GPO, 1971), p. 19.
    a. Crop years beginning: wheat, barley, and oats—July 1; cotton—Aug. 1; corn and grain sorghums—Oct. 1.
    b. Preliminary.

become more effective and the stocks of major commodities—wheat, cotton, and feed grains—have declined (Table 5.6 and Figure 5.2).

The decline in U.S. stocks has been accompanied by the opening of Communist markets of Russia and China for commercial exports (reported grain deals with those countries in 1972). Initially under P.L. 480 surplus agricultural commodities could not be shipped to Communist countries and their satellites. Under these changed circumstances economic and political pressure has been increasing for hardening the terms of P.L. 480 aid. This pressure led to an amendment of P.L. 480 in 1966. This amendment brought down the aid component in food shipments to low levels, and a large debt service burden was created for the recipient countries unlike the aid in the 1950s and early 1960s. In view of a large magnitude of debt service charges for developing countries, the prospects of food aid are bleak, particularly at the present terms of aid. From the U.S. point of view food aid is no longer required to dispose of accumulating surpluses. If food aid is to be given during the next decade or two,

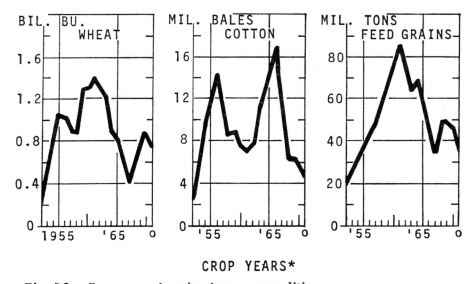

CROP YEARS*

Fig. 5.2.   Carryover of major farm commodities.

Source: U.S. Department of Agriculture, 1971 Handbook of Agricultural Charts, Agricultural Handbook No. 443 (Washington: GPO, Nov. 1971), p. 19.

the United States will have to produce the required quantity instead of
retiring land.

Recipients' Point of View. More and more food aid recipients are reach-
ing a point where they are able to balance their economic demand by domestic supplies. However, despite the rapid increases in agricultural production, many people in these countries do not
have enough income to purchase food, and diets remain nutritionally in-
adequate. This condition can be corrected by increasing the production
of livestock. Food aid with some changes in commodity mix has a large
potential to contribute to additional economic development.

At the same time, however, debt service obligations have reached
critical levels in developing countries, and the situation is not likely to
improve. In view of this problem, there is strong pressure in some countries to stop imports under P.L. 480 (at present terms of aid), despite the
fact that the aid has potential to promote additional employment and
better nutrition. Some countries have stopped food aid; India is one.

SOME POLICY GUIDELINES. The usefulness of food aid as a tool for
economic development during the next decade or two is limited
unless there is a change in the policies of both the United States

and the recipient countries. Some suggestions for changes are as follows:

1. People in the United States understand that food aid can be used as a tool for economic development in LDCs, but this potential cannot be realized at present terms of aid pricing. Food aid commodities can be priced at much lower levels without any additional net cost (the concept used in Chapter 3) to the United States. Such a pricing can improve the aid component in the shipments and preserve the efficacy of food aid as a tool for economic development.

2. The use of food aid for additional development requires an assurance of supplies for a definite number of years. Often recipient countries have considered food aid a lever for political pressure, and it has been subject to political uncertainties. This kind of situation can be improved by channeling the aid commodities through such international organizations as FAO and World Bank.

3. The surplus local currency counterpart funds should be linked with existing projects as and when they accrue if the monetary implications of expenditures from these funds are to be avoided; these funds should be given back in the form of grants if the counterpart fund problem is ever to be solved.

4. Recipient countries should explore the avenues of development through food aid. Employment-generating projects, the livestock industry, and new export outlets are examples of some of the areas that need to be considered. Food aid can be used as an interim measure until domestic supplies become adequate to substitute for imports.

5. To ensure that there are no price dampening impacts on domestic farmers, the recipient countries should be required to channel the aid supplies through differentiated markets. The system of fair-price shops, set up by India, is an example of one way to protect producers.

Review of Related Studies

FOOD AND AGRICULTURE ORGANIZATION PILOT STUDY OF INDIA. In 1955 FAO published a comprehensive study conducted by a team of economists under the leadership of Mordecai Ezekiel to evaluate the alternative uses of surplus commodities to finance economic development. The team conducted the pilot study in India to determine how surplus farm commodities could be used to finance additional investment without competing with sales of domestic products or the usual exports from other countries.

The study outlines four classes of projects in which surplus commodities could be used. Type I projects distribute food as wages-in-kind with all additional food consumed by those receiving the food or their families. Type II projects provide for sale of surplus food on the open market with the proceeds used to employ additional labor on various development projects. Type III projects are similar to Type II except that they offer opportunities for rapid return so proceeds from the project can make it self-supporting or at least cover nonfood expenditures on the project. Projects that fall into this class usually tap reserves of natural resources such as ore or timber. Type IV projects are groups of projects referred to as the program approach. A Type IV program includes the integration of two or more projects as a part of a comprehensive development plan.

Based on a set of assumptions and coefficients for the Indian economy, the study estimates the total need for surplus food as a portion of the total increase in investment through the alternative projects. It concludes that if provisions are made to prevent resale of surplus commodities or substitution of the commodities for domestic purchases, Type I projects could use surplus commodities up to the amount of the total labor cost of the project without depressing food prices.

Based on a Type II project which requires 70% of the total cost as direct labor, and given a marginal propensity to consume food of 0.40 and marketing and transportation costs of surplus food equal to 15 % of the value, direct demand for food equal to only 24% of the project investment would be generated.

Assuming that 10% of the investment is for imported materials and equipment and 20% is for domestic products, additional food demand is generated from the increased income for domestic producers.

(The study points out that additional income can be spent in three ways—more goods sold at the same price, the same amount of goods sold at a higher price, or increased import.)[1] Assuming that allocation of marginal income will be 9% for savings, 9% for taxes, 8% for consumption of imports, and 35% for food purchases (of which 25% is marketing and transportation costs), the 49 units of derived income generate 13 additional units of food demand. Tracing the process through three years, the total demand for additional food reaches only 52% of the initial investment even though direct labor represented 70% of the project costs.

Type III projects are a special case of Type II projects where the project actually finances itself in part or totally after a short initial period of operation. If the project is capable of producing part of its own financing, the amount of capital investment needed is reduced.

Using a Type IV program example requiring 50% of the costs as direct labor, the potential demand for surplus food (assuming the same estimated coefficients as with the Type II project) was estimated to equal 48% of the program investment in the first three years.

The second part of Ezekiel's study was devoted to discussion of specific projects that could be undertaken in India. Projects appropriate for Type I financing include (a) educational food scholarships (particularly for the rural youth and children from low-income families), (b) food scholarships to special groups (i.e., displaced persons and the backward classes such as the primitive and traditional tribes and the religious or social groups affected by prejudices), (c) internships for educated individuals to obtain work experience, (d) village or community development projects (i.e., building schools, wells, village tanks, gutters, dams, access roads, irrigation canals, warehouses, and conservation terraces), and (e) milk marketing schemes (i.e., arrangements for collection, chilling, processing, and shipment of milk; movement of families and their milk animals out of the cities; and supplementing milk supplies with imported milk). Type II examples include road construction, new irrigation projects, reforestation, erosion control, and other development projects that employ unskilled labor. One Type III project that was suggested involved the extension of a road into a virgin forest area and the development of integrated forest industries.

MICHIGAN STATE STUDY OF COLOMBIA. In a study published in 1963, Theodore J. Goering and Lawrence Witt, Michigan State University, analyzed the impact of the P.L. 480 program on the agricultural economy of Colombia.[2] The study considered the potential impact of P.L. 480 imports on four areas of the economy: (1) farm prices, production, and income; (2) economic development and internal resource use; (3) level of consumption of agricultural products; and (4) changes in Colombian foreign exchange expenditures. Comparing domestic prices and production in 1954–55 and 1959–60 of commodities supplied under P.L. 480 agreements with the prices and production of agricultural and nonagricultural commodities not in the program, they concluded that production of wheat increased only slightly over the five-year period while cotton production increased over 25% per year. As with cotton, sesame production increased substantially even though P.L. 480 imports of edible oils (substitute for sesame oil) were large relative to domestic production. The authors concluded that the study shows a strong indication that the national Food Procurement Agency used P.L. 480 wheat imports to satisfy domestic demand at reduced prices rather than undertake a costly price support program which would have stimulated production. At the same time the Food Procurement Agency carried on an active price support program for barley with the apparent impact of shifting domestic production from wheat to barley.

Goering and Witt point out that local currency use can contribute to economic development only if the "appropriate" environment exists—i.e., if resources are available but unemployed because of monetary and fiscal rigidities. They conclude that it is generally agreed that appropriate conditions have prevailed in Colombia (the labor force is increasing faster than the new employment opportunities, creating unemployed resources which have been put to work on development projects financed with P.L. 480 loans) and that the use of local currency has not created undue inflationary pressures on the economy. The Colombian authorities have been uneasy about an annual increase in the price level of under 10%, but this compares favorably with 400% in Brazil, 439% in Argentina, and 1,110% in Chile for the period 1954–60. The study concludes that availability of local currency loans probably was instrumental in stimulating expansion of the total development program in view of the conservative fiscal policy demonstrated in the past.

While the general level of food prices increased by 64% (6% more than general price levels), retail bread price increased 40%, vegetable shortening price increased 117%, and cotton cloth price increased 36%. At the same time P.L. 480 imports of wheat, edible oils, and cotton represented 20%, 11%, and 9% of total supplies respectively. Although P.L. 480 imports may have helped to hold down retail prices, the effect was difficult to measure because of the concurrent influence of domestic price support programs. High support prices may have had an equally significant effect by increasing production and contributing to increased processing efficiency and lower marketing spread through higher volume processing.

The impact of P.L. 480 donation programs was more difficult to evaluate. It was observed that child consultation at health centers decreased by 50% due to CARE school and family feeding activities. School attendance was maintained at unusually high levels by distributing milk, cheese, and rolls.

Observation of market sales before and during large donation programs led the authors to conclude that delivery of surplus commodities to those with nominal purchasing power resulted almost entirely in expanded consumption and not displacement of regular purchases. Consumer purchases in areas with large surplus food programs did not decline in any of the markets after the programs went into effect.

The study points out that an important side effect to the voluntary agency programs may be the development of greater sensitivity by the government to the needs of the destitute and refugee groups. Another side effect may be a shift in tastes and preferences as the result of promotional programs associated with surplus commodity distribution to promote more nutritive diets.

Aggregatively, the authors found that P.L. 480 food programs contributed 52 calories per day to per capita consumption in Colombia. On the average this amounted to a 2.4% increase, but many families were affected much more significantly.

The impact of P.L. 480 shipments on competing third-country trade was the final area examined by Goering and Witt. The authors conclude that strong implications indicate that P.L. 480 has had a negative impact on commercial trade. Peru experienced a fall in cotton exports to Colombia. Since total cotton imports fell, the absolute fall is not proof of negative impact, but Peru's share of the market fell as well. Canadian wheat shipments also have fallen significantly. Their shipments to Colombia fell to only 32% of the preprogram levels, giving a strong indication that the P.L. 480 program did have a negative effect. The authors suggest that this effect might be viewed as Canada's contribution to the development program in Colombia.

USDA STUDY OF UNITED ARAB REPUBLIC. In a study of P.L. 480 in the U.A.R., Umstott concluded that P.L. 480 shipments were closely related to a shift from a 7% cost-of-living increase between 1955 and 1961 to a 5% decrease between 1961 and 1963.[3]

The U.A.R. was producing about 54 percent of its estimated wheat consumption in 1958 when the daily per capita food consumption averaged 2,340 calories. Umstott projected that domestic production would provide less than 44% of the 1966 consumption and that demand for P.L. 480 wheat imports would rise considerably. He concluded that since the agricultural resource base is quite limited in the U.A.R., the government will be forced to look to industrial development as a source of foreign exchange earnings. This will lead to increased employment and directly to greater food demand. Consequently, projections to 1970 indicate an even greater demand for commercial or concessional food imports in the U.A.R.

The impact of Title II and Title III shipments are summarized in terms of program size. Umstott points out that the Title III program in the U.A.R. during 1961–63 was the largest of any recipient country. School feeding under Title III reached about 3 million children.

In addition, P.L. 480 shipments equal to 12% of the total U.A.R. imports in 1961 eased the serious drain on foreign exchange by calling for payment in local currency. Local currency sales allowed the United States to expand its exports significantly to the U.A.R. by overcoming two major obstructions to trade: limited foreign exchange and lack of U.S. demand for U.A.R. commodities. Acceptance of soft currency reduced the need for U.A.R. exchange commodities to supplement foreign exchange purchases.

Using a simple demand prediction equation where change in demand d equals the annual rate of population change p plus the product of the per capita increase in income g and the income elasticity of the demand for food n, Umstott projects a growth in food demand of almost 5% per year.[4] Assuming agricultural output continues to increase at 1% per year, he projected an annual food deficit of 4%.

USDA STUDY OF TURKEY. The team study of Turkey, directed by Resat Aktan, concentrated on the evaluation of the economic impact of P.L. 480 Title I programs through 1962.[5] Two commodity groups constitute most of the program with wheat making up 63%, fats and oils 25%, and various other commodities providing the other 12%.

The study characterizes Turkish agriculture as having traditional production patterns which are hampered by fractionalization of land holdings through inheritance. (Less than 5% of the farmers have a farm wholly in one piece.) Lack of social overhead structures such as credit, transportation, schools, advisory service, and marketing facilities further hinder the transition to a dynamic agriculture. The farmers most involved in the money market are those producing fruits; vegetables; and industrial raw materials such as cotton, tobacco, and oilseeds.

On the basis of price index comparisons, the study concludes that farm prices rose at about the same rate as general prices during the P.L. 480 era and that there is no evidence that P.L. 480 imports had an adverse effect on domestic production of imported products. These results were observed under conditions where annual imports represented the following percentages of domestic production: wheat 1.5–13.5, corn 1.0–6.0, rice 5.0–11.0, and vegetable oils 12.0–60.0.

The researchers observed that official attitudes toward agriculture have not consistently given it priority and integrated programs are needed to make it a significant contributor to economic growth; they concluded that P.L. 480 commodities helped to prevent a major food crisis. The study examines hypothetical production adjustments that might have taken place if P.L. 480 commodities had not been available, but discounts them heavily because of the uncertainty of the direction the government would have moved in the absence of P.L. 480 imports. Downward adjustments must be made on these price estimates to compensate for the one-third to one-half of the local currency proceeds used for U.S. government expenditures. Most of these expenditures would have been made anyway, so dollars would have been available to purchase wheat and vegetable oils commercially and meet part of the food deficit.

The study concludes that many structural changes in demand can be attributed to P.L. 480 imports. The declining price trend for margarine was stabilized by expanded demand. Butter price, in contrast, reversed its rising trend and fell slightly during the 1955–59 period. Agriculture's share of national income declined from 49% before P.L. 480 imports to 40–42% in 1961 and 1962, even though the gross value of production climbed fairly regularly when adjusted for constant prices. Large imports of cereals would have suggested a relative loss by cereal farmers compared with livestock farmers, but the data revealed no evidence for such a conclusion.

Food expenditures were estimated to range between 40 and 70% of consumer budgets for the 1948–62 period, when food consumption was estimated at 2,500–2,800 calories per day. Wheat supplied under P.L. 480 tended to be consumed in the cities and coastal areas; corn and vegetable oils (as margarine) were distributed more evenly over the country. Together the wheat and vegetable oil imports under P.L. 480 represented 10–20% of food expenditures. Complex mixing rates were used to stretch or contract the wheat supply by varying the wheat to rye ratio.

Economic development also reflected the impact of P.L. 480. Investment resulting from P.L. 480 aided in the development of domestic consumer goods industries which replaced imports of many consumer goods. Many of the new industries are still in their infancy, but it appears that they will be able to compete effectively and provide import substitutes in the future. The study concludes that expenditure of local currency increased demand for imports to some degree but did not significantly shift trade patterns.

The researchers observed that P.L. 480 shipments assumed a major role in balancing international accounts. An average of 34.5% of the annual deficit was satisfied with P.L. 480 imports. However, because of large allocations of local currency for U.S. government uses, the net effect on balance of payments must be adjusted downward to account for loss of dollar earnings.

ARIZONA STUDY OF SURPLUS DISPOSAL. A general study of the impact of P.L. 480 on recipient nations was conducted by Elmer Menzie, Lawrence Witt, Carl Eicher, and Jimmye Hillman.[6] The early part of the study points out that a development plan is essentially an investment plan in recipient countries. The greater the food aid program, the more planning is necessary for a unified investment plan.

The study report notes that India moved toward increased P.L. 480 Title I imports because of projected food shortages and lack of foreign exchange to transact commercial purchases. These researchers determined that food would become the limiting factor in the third five-year plan and that domestic resources could be pushed only to the limit of the total food supply. Consequently, large food imports were critical to the success of the development plan.

The case of Title I shipments to Israel differs from many of the other developing countries. Israel already had a per capita income of almost $600 in 1956, a stage of development considerably advanced from that of India and other recipient countries. Limited arable land and high irrigation costs constrained production of wheat and feed grains. P.L. 480 imports of wheat and feed grains permitted a rapid expansion of the livestock industry and aided in relaxation of rationing on eggs, dairy products, meat and poultry. Even dollar aid to Israel would necessarily have been used to purchase increased volumes of feed grains.

Under these conditions P.L. 480 aid served as a close substitute for other forms of financial aid. Although all of the imports did not meet the "additional" condition, consumers benefitted greatly from P.L. 480 imports at the partial expense of commercial exporters in other countries.

The Colombian experience is summarized as resulting in lower wheat prices which caused a shift in production from wheat to barley, as mentioned earlier in the summary of the Goering and Witt study. The shift was made relatively quickly with only slight income effects on Colombian agriculture.

Tunisia is an example of Title II programs that use food as wage payments. Basically, work projects have been designed to develop a social overhead structure of roads, railroads, schools, power plants, and irrigation facilities in rural areas. The work projects originally provided about two-thirds of the salary in food (wheat) and the other third in cash. Part of the cash was spent for additional food and part for nonfood items, creating additional demand for domestic food and nonfood commodities. By November 1961 nearly 200,000 workers were employed full-time on various work projects in Tunisia. Success of the work projects is attributed primarily to the high quality of local planning and administration. Morocco, Afghanistan, Korea, Dahomey, Ethiopia, Iran, Tanganyika, India, and Libya have conducted major work project programs.

The study generalizes the P.L. 480 impact by pointing out that concessional commodity imports appeared to reduce commercial grain imports in Israel and Colombia. The inflow of commodities to Colombia coincided with a sharp drop in world coffee prices and enabled the Colombian government to avoid difficult decisions relating to capital import reductions which would have slowed down development.

The study concludes that for two basic reasons food aid is not a perfect substitute for dollar aid: (1) Most investment programs do not require only wages or labor costs, for which food can be substituted. Normally people need other supplies and equipment which must be purchased with cash. (2) Even if labor represented 100% of the investment costs, marginal preference of the consumer is usually such that additional food demand will not exhaust the wages. In this case part of the surplus food used to finance a given project would find its way into the market system and create a depressing force on domestic prices. Early studies indicated that as high as 50% of additional development costs could be financed with surplus food, but recent studies indicated that the proportion may go as low as 20%.

GOKHALE INSTITUTE STUDY OF INDIA. The Gokhale Institute study of the impact of P.L. 480 assistance on India was published in 1967 by Rath and Patvardhan.[7] The primary purpose of the study was to examine the impact of P.L. 480 imports on consumption, production, and prices of relevant commodities in the domestic market during a crucial period of development from 1956 to 1962.

The first section of the study is devoted to an examination of the role of P.L. 480 assistance in total development expenditures and the impact of its financial operation on the money supply, balance of payments, and trade pattern. The study cites the food policy of India after 1955 as an aim to control food prices sufficiently to avoid undue increases. This policy was implemented by purchasing commodities under P.L. 480 agreements and selling them directly to consumers at fixed prices through fair-price shops. The result has been a reduced price for domestically produced grain in the normal marketing channel and the subsequent continuation of two distinct marketing mechanisms. Most of the P.L. 480 commodities received during this period were a part of the foreign assistance for India's economic development plan. The authors cite the payment for commodities in local currency as "the important feature of these imports." The study summarizes the agreements signed, the accumulation and disposal of accrued funds, the allocation and withdrawal of loan and grant funds, and project statements financed by P.L. 480 loans and grants.

The second section of the study is devoted to an analysis of individual commodity situations, including import accounts, mechanisms and extent of marketing, and building of buffer stocks. The study cites the large imports as a help in holding the increase in cereal prices down to 4% from 1957 to 1962 while the general price level of all commodities increased by 18%. At the same time an attempt to build buffer stocks was falling short of its goal. By the end of 1962 government stocks of food grains stood at 2.3 million metric tons—about 0.4 million metric tons less than in 1960. The authors conclude "that practically all the imported food grains have gone into current consumption."

The third section of the study reviews the food policy from the depression of 1929 to the present. One significant factor in the historical review is the fair-price shop system authorized and established by the Indian government in 1948, roughly six years before the advent of P.L. 480 and the current distribution program. The authors summarize India's food policy from 1956 to 1962 as an attempt to keep food prices steady with a minimum of direct intervention. However, the government exercised numerous indirect controls such as (1) complete ban on exports of cereals after January 1956, (2) importation of food grains (particularly from the United States and Burma) to assist in building a reserve stock, (3) sale of wheat and rice to retail consumers from reserve stocks at fixed prices, (4) selective credit control on advances to traders by banks, (5) regulation of trade by licensing orders, (6) announcement of statutory maximum and minimum prices, and (7) procurement of food grains in surplus states to be sold through the fair-price shops.

The remainder of the study is devoted to an analysis of trends in cereal consumption, prices, and production. The authors cite the release of P.L. 480 wheat as increasing consumption as much as 50% in some states, mostly in urban areas. They also point out the inferiority of P.L. 480 wheat, in the eyes of the Indian consumer, by verifying the negative relationship between income level and purchases at the fair-price shops.

The authors present data to indicate that the purchase of P.L. 480 commodities and their subsequent release at fixed prices from the fair-price shops below the general market level was effective as a policy tool in holding down prices of certain commodities. Wheat prices were controlled almost exclusively by controlling the quantity of P.L. 480 wheat released through the fair-price shops, but imported rice represented a small portion of total consumption and had relatively little effect on rice prices.

Despite the effectiveness of government price control policy, the authors point out that it is difficult to detect any effect of large wheat imports under P.L. 480 on the production of wheat prior to 1962. This conclusion is based primarily on the domination of production by rapid expansion of cultivation to new areas.

The authors conclude by citing the help of P.L. 480 imports in containing the inflationary pressures within the economy, providing substantial additional resources for investment in economic development, and raising the cereal consumption in India. At the same time P.L. 480 imports only slowed inflation rather than stopping it; the imports resulted in increased consumption primarily in urban areas, allowed expanded consumption in middle- and high-income families through consumption of flour mill products, and failed to build buffer stocks because direct sales generated financial resources for planned investment that would not have accrued if the imported commodities had gone into storage.

SUMMARY. This review provides examples of the types of studies undertaken, major issues examined, and the nature of several conclusions reached. It is by no means inclusive of all writings on the impact of P.L. 480. The authors are aware of numerous additional studies dealing with the use of P.L. 480 commodities and related topics. Many of these studies have been cited for particular conceptual or empirical contributions at the appropriate places throughout the book. The literature includes analytical work ranging from theoretical studies (Ezekiel), which attempt to predict aggregative or macroeconomic impacts of P.L. 480 on the recipient economy, to empirical analyses (Umstott), which tend to summarize quantities and values of commodities only to place them in perspective with related consumption and production data for the recipient economy. The bulk of studies lie between these two points. Most of them develop theoretical concepts based on bits of empirical data from one country (or a few countries) to test hypotheses based on established theory.

The major issues developed in the literature center around two aspects of food aid programs—the commodity impact and the local currency impact. We have subdivided the analyses of these topics into controversies over consumption (improving minimum diet levels, allocation of marginal income, matching commodity aid with commodity demand, wages-in-kind, and shifts in consumption patterns), prices (responsiveness of consumers and producers, desirable wholesale and retail price levels, and control of price fluctuations), production (competition with domestic producers, resource allocation, import substitution, and productivity of capital), and trade (maintenance of normal patterns, balance-of-payments benefits, and potential markets). Closely related topics explored within this framework include changes in levels of investment, employment, income, inflation, tax revenue, and debt accumulation.

In general we have come to the conclusion that P.L. 480 commodities do substitute for a portion of foreign aid to many developing countries without serious adverse effects. Estimates of the rate of substitution vary considerably between countries, or even within countries under alternative assumptions. We also concluded that requirements for the use of surplus commodities to promote economic development without adversely disrupting the recipient economy are: (1) the availability of idle resources which can be mobilized through the use of food aid, (2) the capability of matching commodity aid with derived consumer demand, and (3) the availability of supporting capital—domestic or foreign—to finance nonfood expenses and satisfy effective nonfood demand.

The Ezekiel study represented a systematic attempt to integrate the theoretical concepts of food aid with empirical data to predict the impact of P.L. 480 shipments on the recipient economy. The research team conducted the analysis with a limited amount of data and knowledge of the scope of P.L. 480 operations. As a consequence the study is generally limited to predictions based on one set of parameters for consumption and production response. In classifying projects as isolated activities, the Ezekiel research team underestimated the total contribution of Type I, II, and III projects to the growth of the general economy by virtually ignoring the investment contribution of the projects to domestic production. They mentioned this aspect later when they discussed the program approach to uses of food aid. Given the limited time available and the major concentration on predicting the amount of food that could be used for specific types of projects, the report of the Ezekiel study did not analyze project-related variables such as the magnitudes of supporting capital needs, derived demand for nonfood commodities, tax revenue, investment, and employment.

The Rath and Patvardhan study attempted to estimate the impact of P.L. 480 imports on production, prices, and consumption. But instead of examining the possible potential use of food aid, their study concentrates only on summarizing historical data and hypothesizing relationships. To make a real contribution the study should have estimated food demand, production, deficits or surpluses at government controlled prices, the role of food aid in meeting deficits, impact of P.L. 480 sales on the monetary sector, and impact of P.L. 480 imports on trade. While informative, the historical approach taken in the study only begins to answer the crucial questions about P.L. 480 programming—those relating to the impact of stimulating rapid economic development in developing countries.

The remaining studies dealt with concepts more within a microeconomic framework. They placed their emphasis on analysis of producer and consumer response to conditions that prevailed during periods of food aid imports in an attempt to predict anticipated response under alternative conditions. In effect these studies provide the parameters for the broader analysis of impact on the agricultural sector and general economy.

India and the P.L. 480 Program

S I N C E India has been extensively used as an illustrative case, it seems appropriate to present some details of P.L. 480 operations there. During the first five-year plan (1951–52 to 1955–56) food imports were rendered unnecessary (except during the year 1951–52) due to a bumper agricultural production within the country and the modest size of the plan. But right from the beginning of the second plan (1956–57 to 1960–61) food imports became a must, due to the magnitude of plan investment. The plan emphasized heavy and basic industries in the face of growing foreign exchange shortage and lagging agricultural production, and the government of India was compelled to enter into an agreement with the United States. Since then and until March 1969 the two countries signed a number of further agreements and supplementaries. The brief details are presented in Table B.1.

During the years between 1955–56 and 1968–69, $4,388.366 million worth of agricultural commodities were programmed to be shipped to India under the fourteen agreements. Of these agreements the fifth one (May 4, 1960) is of special significance since it was the largest in absolute terms and, unlike later agreements, for a four-year period. Since the signing of the agreement coincided with the preparation of the third five-year plan (1961–62 to 1965–66), it went a long way to provide a perspective for enhanced development efforts. The last four agreements contained an increasing proportion of aid repayable in dollars under Title IV instead of rupees under Title I.

Among the commodities imported under Title I are wheat, rice, maize, milo, cotton, dairy products, tobacco, and soybean oil. The product mix of Title I has been such that wheat is the most prominent commodity. Commodity composition of the P.L. 480 agreements is presented in Table B.3.

Throughout the program period analyzed here, wheat shipments have been about 66.72% of the total shipments in value terms. Other major commodities are cotton, feed grains, and rice with 8.88, 6.26, and 4.93% respectively.

PROGRAMMED ALLOCATION OF P.L. 480 COUNTERPART

FUNDS. All the local currency repayable agreements program the allocation of the counterpart funds among the various uses

TABLE B.1. P.L. 480 Agreements between India and the United States through March 3, 1969

Serial No. 1	Date of Agreement 2	Commodities 3	Value ($ million) 4
1	8/29/56 as amended	Wheat, rice, cotton, dairy products	354.556
2	6/23/58	Wheat, yellow corn, sorghum	55.277
3	9/26/58	Wheat, yellow corn	259.800
4	11/13/59 as amended	Wheat, rice, milo, corn, cotton, tobacco	297.870
5	5/4/60 as amended	Wheat, rice, milo, corn, cotton, tobacco, soybean oil	1,369.800
6	5/1/62 as amended	Cotton, yellow corn, tobacco	39.300
7	11/26/62 as amended	Cotton, maize, tobacco	103.100
8	11/30/62	Milk, powder, cheese, canned fruit	5.103
9	9/30/64 as amended	Wheat, rice, milo, vegetable oil, lubricants, cotton, maize, tobacco	1,187.360
10	2/20/67	Wheat, wheat flour, soybeans, tallow, soybean oil	135.000
11	6/24/67	Wheat, sorghum, milo, soybean oil	87.800
12	9/12/67 (supplementary)	Wheat, sorghum, soybean oil, cotton	67.500
13	12/30/67	Wheat, sorghum	168.600
14	12/23/68	Wheat, tallow, cotton, tobacco, nonfat dry milk	95.500
		Total	4,226.566

Source: P.L. 480 Branch, Ministry of Finance, Government of India; Government of India, External Assistance (New Delhi, 1968), pp. 113–14.

mentioned in Section 104 of the P.L. 480 Act. All the uses listed in Section 104 can be grouped into five broad categories:

1. Common defense (Section 104e).
2. Grants for economic development of the recipient countries (Section 104e).
3. Loans to the recipient governments (Section 104f).

TABLE B.2.   Convertible Currency Portion of Agreements

Agreement	Date of Agreement	Commodities	Value ($ million)
1	6/24/67	Wheat, wheat flour	24.200
2	9/12/67	Wheat, wheat flour	19.000
3	12/30/67	Wheat, wheat flour	46.900
4	12/23/68	Wheat, tallow, cotton, tobacco, nonfat dry milk	71.600
		Total	161.700

Source: Government of India, External Assistance (New Delhi, 1968), pp. 113–14.

4. U.S. uses (Section 104a, b, c, d, h, i, j, k, l, m, n, o, p, q, r, s, t, and so on).

5. Loans to private enterprise (the Cooley Amendment of 1958) to be disbursed out of the counterpart funds in the recipient country.

The Agricultural Trade Development and Assistance Act, 1954 (P.L. 480), page 5, states:

For promoting balanced economic development and trade among nations, for which purposes no more than 25 percent of the currencies received pursuant to each such agreement shall be available through and the procedures established by the Export-Import Bank for loans mutually agreeable to said bank

TABLE B.3.   Commodity Components of P.L. 480 Agreements

Commodity	Unit	Quantity (million)	Value ($ million)	Percent
Wheat	metric ton	45,912	2,816.4	66.72
Food grains	metric ton	5,242	264.4	6.26
Rice	metric ton	1,748	208.1	4.93
Cotton	Indian bales	3,258	374.7	8.88
Tallow	metric ton	0,080	15.4	0.36
Nonfat dairy milk	metric ton	0,007	16.6	0.39
Soybean/vegetable oil	metric ton	0,021	3.6	0.08
Evaporated milk	metric ton	0,297	74.6	1.78
Whole milk powder	metric ton	neg.	0.3	.01
Cheese (processed)	metric ton	neg.	0.1	.00
Canned fruit	metric ton	neg.	0.1	.00
Total market value			3,778.4	89.50
Ocean transportation			443.5	10.50
Total including ocean transportation			4,221.2	100.00

Source: Government of India, External Assistance (New Delhi, 1968), p. 115.
Note: This does not include the commodities under convertible currency agreements as the commodity breakdown is not available.

and the country with which the agreement is made, to United States business firms, and branches, subsidiaries or affiliates of such firms, for business development and trade expansion in such countries, and for loans to domestic or foreign firms for establishment of facilities for aiding in the utilization, distribution, or otherwise increasing the consumption of, and markets for United States agricultural products: Provided, however, that no such loans shall be made for the manufacture of any products to be exported to United States in competition with products produced in United States or for manufacture or production of any commodity to be marketed in competition with United States agricultural commodities or the products thereof. Foreign currencies may be accepted in repayment of such loans.

In India the common defense section has never been applied. The allocation of the counterpart funds has been among the last four types of uses mentioned. A noteworthy point in Table B.4 is that the grant content as been falling in later agreements, and many agreements do not carry any grant element at all. Meanwhile the loan portion has been going up, and it has gone as high as 87% in recent agreements. The implication of increased loan content is that repayment will continue for long after the actual imports have ceased. This aspect has been discussed in Chapter 4. Over the period as a whole the programmed earmarking for the four types of uses were:

1. Loans to GOI—60.58%
2. Grants to GOI—19.76%
3. U.S. uses—13.12%
4. Cooley loans—6.55%

TECHNIQUE OF P.L. 480 OPERATION IN INDIA. The entire operation (exports from United States and imports in India) under P.L. 480 involves numerous transactions from the signing of agreements to the final disposal of commodities in India to the disbursement of counterpart funds for various earmarked uses in India. The stepwise transactions are shown in Figure B.1.

1. **Signing of Agreement.** Under Title I of the P.L. 480 program an agreement must be signed first between the Government of India and the United States. The agreement specifies the terms of sale, the maximum value in dollars, exchange rate between the rupee and dollar, the approximate quantity of commodities to be purchased under the agreement, and earmarkings of counterpart funds for four types of uses mentioned. The size of the agreement depends on the request submitted by the GOI to the USDA. It is reviewed by USDA and submit-

TABLE B.4. Programmed Allocations of P.L. 480 Counterpart Funds

Date of Agreement	Loans to GOI	Percentage of Total	Grants to GOI	Percentage of Total	Retained for U.S. Uses	Percentage of Total	Cooley Amendment Loans	Percentage of Total	Total Amount
8/29/56	226.256	63.81	54.000	15.23	74.300	20.96	...	...	354.556
6/30/58	33.377	69.38	...	...	8.081	14.62	13.819	25.00	55.277
9/26/58	129.700	49.92	37.500	14.42	27.600	10.63	65.000	25.02	259.800
11/13/59	119.100	39.98	119.100	39.98	44.740	15.02	14.930	5.02	297.870
5/4/60	577.565	42.16	577.565	41.16	146.115	10.67	65.555	5.01	1,369.800
5/1/62	34.977	89.00	...	...	3.930	10.00	0.393	1.00	39.300
11/26/62	87.635	85.00	...	...	10.310	10.00	5.155	5.00	103.100
11/30/62	4.338	85.00	...	...	0.510	10.00	0.255	5.00	5.103
9/30/64	911.890	77.70	...	...	194.780	10.00	80.740	7.70	1,187.360
2/20/63	87.750	65.00	29.700	22.00	10.800	14.60	6.750	5.00	135.000
6/24/67	76.386	87.91	...	...	7.024	8.00	4.390	4.99	87.800
9/12/67	58.725	87.00	...	...	5.400	8.00	3.375	5.00	67.500
12/30/67	146.682	87.00	...	...	13.488	8.00	8.430	5.00	168.600
12/23/68	66.000	69.12	17.500	18.32	7.000	7.33	5.000	5.24	995.500
Total	2,560.38	60.58	835.365	19.76	554.028	13.12	276.792	6.55	4,226.566

Source. Government of India, External Assistance (New Delhi, 1968), pp. 113–14.

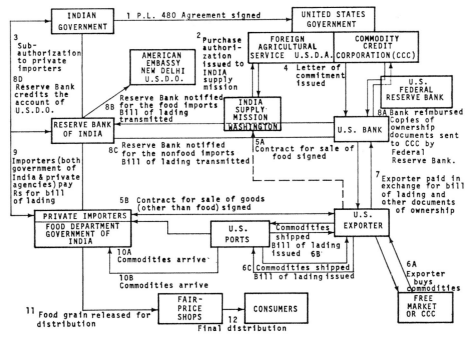

Fig. B.1. Technique of P.L. 480 operations.

ted as a proposal to the Interagency Staff Committee in Washington, D.C., which in turn analyzes, modifies, accepts, or rejects the submitted proposal. Finally an agreement is signed to this effect.

2. **Issue of Purchase Authorization.** Then the commodities are to be bought. A purchase authorization is necessary for this purpose, and a request for purchase authorization is sent through the India Supply Mission in Washington to the U.S. Foreign Agricultural Service, which issues a purchase authorization to the mission. The purchase authorization specifically mentions the grade or type of commodities to be purchased (such as U.S. No. 1 Hard Red Winter Wheat), approximate quantity of commodities, and the period within which purchases are to be effected. The total dollar amount of the program authorized by a commodity agreement is split into a number of purchase authorizations from time to time depending on the availability of surplus commodities.

3. **Issue of Subauthorization.** Food content—i.e., wheat, rice, maize, and
    milo—is imported by the GOI so the purchase authorizations are
    used by the India Supply Mission itself. Other commodities
such as cotton, tobacco, and dairy products are imported by private firms.
For them the GOI issues subauthorizations under the purchase authorization received by its agency (India Supply Mission, Washington). The
subauthorization designates the bank(s) in the United States and Reserve
Bank of India to handle the transactions.

4. **Letter of Commitment.** The India Supply Mission requests the Com-
    modity Credit Corporation (CCC) to issue a letter of commit-
    ment to the bank(s) designated by it to handle the concerned
transactions. The letter of commitment is the confirmation by CCC to
reimburse the designated U.S. bank(s) that will handle the U.S. exports
to India. The U.S. bank(s) accepts the commitment, and the Federal Reserve Bank of the United States acts as a banker to CCC.

5A. **Signing of Contract between India Supply Mission and U.S. Ex-
    porters.** The India Supply Mission, Washington, enters into an
    agreement with U.S. exporters for the supply of wheat, rice,
maize, and milo at prices agreed upon between the U.S. supplier and
the mission. Later the United States submits this agreement along with
other documents to the U.S. bank(s) as per letter of commitment, for
the receipt of payment in dollars.

5B. **Signing of Contract between Indian Private Importers and U.S.
    Exporters.** The private firms which have been issued sub-
    authorization by the GOI choose their suppliers for the com-
modities mentioned therein. The supplier has to present the contract to
the U.S. bank(s) as in the case of the Supply Mission in order to receive
the necessary payments.

6A, B. **Purchase of Commodities.** A U.S. supplier may purchase the
    commodity either from the regular market or from CCC. Be-
    cause U.S. prices are higher than world prices, the difference
has to be met by a USDA export subsidy. The next step is to arrange
the shipping of the food products by the India Supply Mission. The
shipping of commodities is arranged by the importers or their agents in
the case of FOB (free on board) shipments and by U.S. exporters in the
case of CIF (cost, insurance, and freight) shipments. In both cases the
shipping companies deliver the bill of lading to the U.S. exporter.

TABLE B.5. Entries Relating to P.L. 480 Transactions in Central Government Budget

Item	Credit Entry in Budget	Debit Entry in Budget
1. Payments to U.S. for food imports	Gross investment of P.L. 480 deposits in special securities	Capital outlay on schemes of government trading
2. Payments to U.S. account for nonfood grain imports	Gross investment of P.L. 480 deposits in special securities	
3. P.L. 480 grants	Extraordinary receipts	Disinvestment of special securities
4. P.L. 480 loans	Public debt—debt raised outside India	Disinvestment of special securities
5. Payment for transport not covered in (1)		Capital outlay on schemes of government trading
6. Interest payments on P.L. 480 loans, special securities	Since 1964–65: gross investment in special securities	Debt services
7. Expenditure on P.L. 480 projects		Amount debited from Special Development Fund gross when credit is taken for SDF net in the budget
8. P.L. 480 loans	Special Development Fund (gross)	Capital Head 128—transfer of development assistance from U.S.A.
9. P.L. 480 grants	Special Development Fund (gross)	Extraordinary charges—transfer of P.L. 480 grants to Special Development Fund
10. Repayment of P.L. 480 loans		Repayment of debt
11. Transfer of funds from SBI	Gross investment of P.L. 480 deposits in special securities	
12. Proceeds of sale of P.L. 480 food	Amount deducted from gross outlays on schemes of government trading	
13. U.S. expenditure out of counterpart funds including Cooley loans and loans and grants to Nepal and Burma		Disinvestment of special securities

Source: K. Sundaram, "The Relationship between P.L. 480 Transactions, Money, Supply with Public and Prices: An Analysis," p. 91.

7. **Payments to Exporters.** U.S. exporters receive payment on presentation of contract(s) and bill of lading to the U.S. bank(s) mentioned in the letter of commitment. Exporters are paid in dollars by the U.S. bank(s).

8A, B, C, D. **Bank Transactions.** The documents thus received by the U.S. bank are in turn presented to the Federal Reserve Bank of the United States (which is banker to CCC), and payment is made in dollars. Then the U.S. bank notifies and sends the bill of lading to the India Supply Mission regarding food grains purchased. The India Supply Mission informs and sends the bill of lading to the Reserve Bank of India. In case of nonfood content of P.L. 480 aid, the U.S. bank directly notifies the RBI, which credits the account of the U.S. Disbursing Office to itself as soon as it is paid for obtaining the bill of lading.

9. **Rupee Payment by GOI and Other Importers.** Both the GOI and private importers obtain a bill of lading and pay in rupees to RBI in the U.S. Disbursing Office account.

10. **Commodities Arrive at Indian Ports.** Food grain shipments are received by the agencies of the GOI. Nonfood items are received on the basis of the bill of lading by private importers.

11 and 12. **Release of Commodities to Consumers through Fair-Price Shops.** Food grains thus imported are released directly through the agency of fair-price shops. A small part of the commodities is sold after the processing through flour mills has been completed.

BUDGET ENTRIES RELATING TO P.L. 480 TRANSACTIONS.

For analytical exposition of Chapter 4, the procedure of recording the P.L. 480 transactions in the budget of the GOI may be briefly summed up. This is presented in tabular form (Table B.5).

Recently, in accordance with the recommendations of the Khusro Panel Report, all the transactions relating to P.L. 480 operations have been consolidated in one single account in the budget papers of the GOI.[1] This presentation is very close to the concept of net support of P.L. 480 counterpart funds developed in Chapter 4 of this study.

A P P E N D I X C

Basic Data Tables

TABLE C.1. Basic Data (Annual Values) of Variables

Year	Q_t^s	Q_t^d	Q_t^c	Y_t	M_t^o	W_t	P_{t-2}^c	P_t^c	R_{t-1}	T_{t-1}	P_t^r	P_t^p	M_t^p	C_t^p	G_t
1956	126.5	126.3	5.2	243.57	3.3	−1.5	84.0	89.3	109.24	639	100.29	97.09	0.37	0.09	8,271.84
1957	129.8	129.1	7.5	255.70	2.2	2.1	79.3	93.6	118.95	664	101.01	91.74	6.76	0.31	10,954.13
1958	119.1	117.9	9.6	247.68	3.2	−0.7	89.3	94.6	84.74	630	104.77	90.09	4.62	0.57	11,423.42
1959	135.4	131.1	12.2	256.60	1.9	1.2	93.6	89.6	100.62	707	109.14	86.21	7.48	2.13	9,818.97
1960	131.2	128.4	11.4	243.32	2.1	3.2	94.6	85.4	106.17	713	105.04	81.30	9.95	1.70	10,845.53
1961	137.0	136.3	9.0	253.67	2.9	−0.4	89.6	81.0	101.65	753	104.05	79.37	5.22	0.53	11,603.17
1962	129.4	136.2	9.6	256.67	1.9	−0.8	85.4	83.5	99.88	763	107.64	78.74	6.37	0.40	14,748.03
1963	129.4	128.1	11.2	251.16	0.9	−0.1	81.0	84.1	93.50	733	110.98	75.76	9.01	0.44	18,098.48
1964	129.9	127.5	18.2	244.56	2.0	2.6	83.5	90.5	95.98	757	113.45	67.57	11.40	1.45	17,141.89
1965	138.3	130.5	20.7	260.16	2.7	−2.2	84.1	90.1	104.80	816	111.12	64.28	12.86	4.83	16,490.68
1966	109.1	101.4	28.2	225.52	7.9	−0.3	90.5	90.2	74.10	683	111.37	77.62	12.96	6.57	16,601.09
1967	112.0	104.5	25.8	217.72	9.2	−0.5	90.1	97.6	88.38	707	121.27	69.16	7.93	6.77	15,405.66

Sources: Government of India, *Economic Survey 1969–70* (New Delhi: 1970); Directorate of Economics and Statistics, Ministry of Food and Agriculture, *Bulletin of Food Statistics* (New Delhi: GOI, 1956–1970); Office of Agricultural Attaché, American Embassy, *Brief on Indian Agriculture 1970* (New Delhi: U.S. Embassy, 1969–70); Ralph W. Cummings, Jr. and S. K. Ray, "Relative Contribution of Weather and New Technology," *Economic and Political Weekly* 48(Sept. 1969):A163–A174; Directorate of Economics and Statistics, Ministry of Food, Agriculture, Community Development and Cooperation, *Estimates of Area and Production of Principal Crops in India 1968–69*, Summary Tables (New Delhi: GOI, 1969).

TABLE C.2. Sale Proceeds of P.L. 480 Title I Imports on GOI Account

Year	Total Wheat Releases from Central Stocks (000 metric tons)	Percentage of P.L. 480	P.L. 480 Sales (000 metric tons)	Issue Price for Metric Ton (Rs crores)	Sale Proceeds of Wheat (Rs crores)	Total Rice Released from Central Stocks (000 metric tons)	Percentage of P.L. 480	P.L. 480 Rice Sales (000 metric tons)	Issue Price of Rice per Metric Ton (Rs crores)	Sale Proceeds of Rice (Rs crores)	Sale Proceeds of Other Grains (Rs crores)	Total Proceeds (Rs crores)
1956-57	1,514	43.85[a]	663.9	375.1	24.90	787	5.64[c]	44.3	482.3	2.14	...	27.04
1957-58	2,435	86.11[b]	2,097.6	375.1	78.68	746	5.64[c]	42.1	482.3	2.03	...	80.71
1958-59	3,381	86.11[b]	2,911.4	375.1	109.21	750	5.64[c]	42.3	482.3	2.04	neg.	111.25
1959-60	3,324	86.11[b]	2,862.3	375.1	107.36	1,022	5.64[c]	57.6	482.3	2.78	neg.	110.14
1960-61	3,434	86.11[b]	2,957.0	375.1	110.92	881	20.73[d]	182.6	482.3	8.81	neg.	119.73
1961-62	2,858	86.11[b]	2,361.0	375.1	88.56	695	20.73[d]	144.1	482.3	5.94	neg.	94.50
1962-63	3,207	86.11[b]	2,761.5	375.1	103.58	1,003	20.73[d]	207.3	482.3	10.00	neg.	113.58
1963-64	4,814	86.11[b]	4,145.3	375.1	155.49	1,149	20.73[d]	238.2	482.3	11.49	...	166.98
1964-65 to 12/31/64	5,105	86.11[b]	4,395.0	375.1	164.89	1,166	20.73[d]	240.7	482.3	11.61	...	240.34
From 1/1/65 to 11/16/65	1,337	86.11[b]	1,151.3	482.5	55.55	563	20.73[d]	116.7	710.0	8.29	...	...
1965-66 to 11/16/65	4,232	86.11[b]	3,644.2	482.5	175.83	2,016	20.73[d]	417.9	710.0	29.67	...	320.72
From 11/17/65 to 1966	2,676	86.11[b]	2,304.3	500.0	115.22	...	...	...	...	...	...	...
1966-67	8,142	...	6,467.2	530.0[e]	348.26	4,131	...	...	...	...	76.03	424.29
1967-68	7,366	...	4,055.1	550.0[e]	226.61	3,010	...	...	...	...	91.08	317.69
1968-69	5,746	...	3,902.0	685.0[e]	271.58	3,584	...	...	...	...	27.43	299.01

Sources: Total release from central stock (financial year basis except for last 3 years) and P.L. 480 import figures (financial year basis) are from the Ministry of Food and Agriculture, GOI. Issue prices are from *Bulletin of Food Statistics*, GOI, 1962-66.

Notes: a. Percentage of P.L. 480 to total availability in central stocks (imports and old stocks).
b. Average of P.L. 480 imports to total availability in central stocks (imports and old stocks).
c. Average of first four years to total availability in central stock imports plus internal procurement. This method takes into account the stocking and destocking automatically.
d. Figures of the first years have been separately averaged to find the proportion of P.L. 480 in central stock.
e. Prices have been changed several times so an average has been taken here.

TABLE C.3.   Incidental Charges of P.L. 480 Title I

Year	Wheat Imports (000 metric tons)	Rice Imports (000 metric tons)	Other Grain Imports (000 metric tons)	Total Imports (000 metric tons)	Incidental Charges (per metric ton, Rs)	Total Incidental Charges (Rs crores)
1956–57	724	65	...	789	49.7	3.92
1957–58	2,461	132	76	2,593	49.7	12.89
1958–59	2,445	...	55	2,521	49.7	12.53
1959–60	2,876	9	26	2,940	49.3	14.49
1960–61	4,098	356	37	4,480	67.3	30.15
1961–62	1,842	183	10	2,062	74.2	15.30
1962–63	3,003	194	...	3,207	87.5	28.06
1963–64	4,138	367	...	2,505	86.8	39.10
1964–65	5,458	232	96	5,690	86.8	49.38
1965–66	6,378	205	1,592	6,679	86.8	57.97
1966–67	6,467	...	1,907	8,059	86.8[a]	69.96
1967–68	4,055	...	482	5,962	86.8[a]	51.75
1968–69	3,902	...	...	4,384	86.8[a]	38.05

Source: Incidental average charges per metric ton are from Ministry of Food and Agriculture, GOI.
a. Figures not available; hence 1965–66 value extended.

TABLE C.4. U.S. Use Expenditures

Period	Amount
	(Rs 000)
Cumulative through 6/30/62	343,091
Fiscal year ending 6/30/63	123,258
Fiscal year ending 6/30/64	148,332
Fiscal year ending 6/30/65	166,111
Fiscal year ending 6/30/66	226,651
Fiscal year ending 6/30/67	267,997
Fiscal year ending 6/30/68	311,443
Fiscal year ending 6/30/69	445,412[a]
Cumulative through 6/30/69	2,032,295

Source: Office of the Financial Attaché, U.S. Embassy, New Delhi, India.

Note: In addition to the U.S. Embassy's expenditures in India, this includes third-country assistance, emergency relief to the GOI, and special loans and grants to the GOI.

a.   This includes a grant of Rs 105 million to the Electrification Corporation.

TABLE C.5. Basic Data at Current and Constant (1960–61) Prices (Rs crores)

	1957–58	1958–59	1959–60	1960–61	1961–62	1962–63	1963–64	1964–65	1965–66	1966–67	1967–68
1. GNP											
Current prices	a	a	a	14,044	14,874	15,821	18,113	21,198	21,799	25,002	29,377
1960–61 prices	11,978	12,920	13,162	14,044	14,579	14,952	15,803	16,930	16,053[b]	16,233[b]	17,622[b]
2. Exports of commodities and services											
Current prices	823	736	793	800	815	846	997	1,029	968	1,342	1,517
1960–61 prices	823	809	793	800	824	883	1,049	1,061	939	872	985
3. Imports of commodities and services (M)											
Current prices	1,332	1,140	1,048	1,266	1,180	1,296	1,364	1,649	1,596	2,249	2,447
1960–61 prices	1,211	1,096	927	1,266	1,157	1,323	1,450	1,603	1,478	1,415	1,772
4. Minimum requirement of import of commodities and services (M)											
Current prices	757	594	701	825	840	861	902	892	936	1,184	1,348
1960 61 prices	701	585	671	825	832	905	944	915	890	774	1,009

Sources: 1. Central Stastistical Organization White Paper, Mar. 1969.
2, 3, 4. Basic data statistics relating to the Indian economy from RBI Bulletins.
a. Revised series of GNP at current prices not available for pre-1960–61 years.
b. Provisional figures.

NOTES

CHAPTER ONE

1. This aspect of the food aid has been highlighted in all the case studies undertaken thus far. See Fanny Ginor, *Use of Agriculture Surpluses*, pp. 147–61; Christopher Beringer and Irshad Ahmad, *Use of Agricultural Surplus Commodities for Economic Development in Pakistan* (Karachi: Institute of Development Economics, 1964), pp. 18–20; Lawrence Witt and Carl Eicher, *The Effects of United States Agricultural Surplus Disposal Program on the Recipient Countries*, p. 13.

2. U.S. Statutes at Large 80, P.L. 436, 1968, p. 450.

3. V. K. R. V. Rao, "Investment, Income and Multiplier in an Underdeveloped Economy," in A. N. Agarwala and S. P. Singh (eds.), *The Economics of Underdevelopment* (London: Oxford University Press, 1958), p. 209.

4. Robert I. McKinnan, "Foreign Exchange Constraint in Economic Development and Efficient Aid Allocation," *Econ. J.* 74 (June 1966): 388–409.

5. Organization for Economic Cooperation and Development, *Foreign Aid Policies Reconsidered* (Paris: OECD, 1966), p. 78.

6. T. W. Schultz, "Value of U.S. Farm Surpluses to Underdeveloped Countries," *J. Farm Econ.* 42 (Dec. 1960): 1028.

7. Dharam Narain and V. K. R. V. Rao, *Foreign Aid and India's Economic Development*, Occasional Paper No. 3 (New Delhi: Institute of Economic Growth, 1963), p. 66.

8. FAO/UN, *The Linking of Food Aid with Other Aid*, p. 21.

9. The Engel curve and the food consumption function are closely related since they are both measures of the same basic relationship. Either curve can be derived directly from the other. Derivation of the consumption curve from the double log Engel curve: log (percent food) $=$ log a $+$ b log (total expenditure) or log (food expenditure/total expenditure) $=$ log a $+$ b (total expenditure), which can be written log (food expenditure) $-$ log (total expenditure) $=$ a $+$ b log (total expenditure); therefore log (food expenditure) $=$ log a $+$ (b $+$ 1) log (total expenditure), which is the double log form of the consumption function.

10. Hendrik S. Houthakker, "An International Comparison of Household Expenditure Patterns, Commemorating the Centenary of Engel's Law," *Econometrica* 25 (Oct. 1957): 532–51.

11. Total expenditures differ from disposable income by the amount of savings and hoarding. Since income elasticities are normally smaller than expenditure elasticities, formulation of the test with income would only further emphasize the results obtained from using expenditures for the associated income levels.

12. Regression of the percentage of budget spent for food on total expenditure directly fits a linear relationship with a constant slope, which implies a constant change in food consumption with respect to a change in expenditure (i.e., constant marginal propensity to consume food) and assumes that the coefficient of elasticity tends toward unity as income increases indefinitely. The linear form is inconsistent with consumer behavior by precluding the asymptotic approach to a plateau of maximum consumption. Regression of the log of the percentage of budget spent for food on the log of total expenditure fits a double-log relationship which implies constant elasticity.

The double-log form is often rejected on the basis of empirical evidence denying constant elasticity of demand for food. This form is probably used more often than the functional form merits, simply because the elasticity coefficient is determined directly as the regression coefficient. The double-log form is often satisfactory over a relatively narrow income range, particularly when food consumption is expressed in terms of expenditure rather than as marginal propensity to consume or constant elasticity and allows the elasticity to vary with level of expenditure.

13. John W. Mellor, *The Economics of Agricultural Development*, p. 62.

14. Robert D. Stevens, *Elasticity of Food Consumption Associated with Changes in Income in Developing Countries*, p. 18.

15. National Council of Applied Economic Research, *All-India Consumer Expenditure Survey*, New Delhi, June 1967.

16. Ki Hyuk Pak and Kee Chun Hau, *Analysis of Food Consumption in the Republic of Korea*, p. 77.

17. L. M. Goreux, "Income and Food Consumption," *FAO Monthly Bull.* 9 (Oct. 1960): 6.

18. Ansley J. Coale and Edgar M. Hoover, *Population Growth and Economic Development in Low-Income Countries* (Princeton, N.J.: Princeton University Press, 1958), p. 125.

19. Stevens, p. 19.

20. Ibid., p. 24.

21. Mellor, p. 78.

22. Bruce F. Johnston and John W. Mellor, "The Role of Agriculture in Economic Development," *Am. Econ. Rev.* 51 (Sept. 1961): 566–93.

23. Results of the Indian study were observed to be unusually low estimates compared to the other studies and therefore are omitted. The low estimates may be attributed to the collection of data through budget studies which previously have been identified as tending to provide low estimates.

24. Stevens's estimated Engel curve is $F/E = 116.83 - 29.34 \log E$.

25. FAO/UN, *Use of Agricultural Surpluses to Finance Economic Development in Underdeveloped Countries*, p. 9.

26. Ibid.

27. Stevens, p. 19.

28. FAO/UN, *Use of Agricultural Surpluses*, p. 9.

CHAPTER TWO

1. T. W. Schultz, "Value of U.S. Farm Surpluses to Underdeveloped Countries," *J. Farm Econ.* 42 (Dec. 1960): 1019–30.

2. See Keith D. Rogers, Uma K. Srivastava, and Earl O. Heady, "Modified Price, Production and Income Impacts of Food Aid under Market Differentiated Distribution," *Am. J. Agr. Econ.* 54 (May 1972): 201–8.

3. Theodore W. Schultz, *Transforming Traditional Agriculture*, p. 131.

4. Ibid., p. 145.

5. U. K. Srivastava, Robert W. Crown, and Earl O. Heady, "Green Revolution and Farm Income Distribution," *Economic and Political Weekly* 6 (Dec. 25, 1971): A163–A172. For a classification of innovations in agriculture, see Earl O. Heady, "Basic Economic and Welfare Aspects of Farm Technological Advance," *J. Farm Econ.* 21 (May 1949): 293–316.

6. For a discussion of impact of relative profitability and fertilizer use in a developing country, see Willis Peterson and Darrell Fienup, "The Economics of Nitrogen Fertilization of Corn in Argentina," unpublished paper, University of Chicago, June 1972.

7. Jitendar S. Mann, "The Impact of Public Law 480 Imports on Prices and Domestic Supply of Cereals in India," *J. Farm Econ.* 49 (Feb. 1967): 131–46.

8. Franklin M. Fisher, "A Theoretical Analysis of the Impact of Food Surplus

Disposal on Agricultural Production in Recipient Countries," *J. Farm Econ.* 45 (Nov. 1963): 863–75.

9. Government of India, *Report of the Study Team on Fair-Price Shops*, p. 3.

10. M_t^p (per capita P.L. 480 imports in kg) and d_t^c (per capita issues from fair-price shops in kg) are as follows for the years 1956–1967:

	1956	1957	1958	1959	1960	1961	1962	1963	1964	1965	1966	1967
M_t^p	0.39	6.70	4.85	7.53	10.03	5.27	6.37	8.60	10.73	12.46	16.81	12.23
d_t^c	5.23	7.52	9.61	12.19	11.40	8.99	9.64	11.17	18.24	20.70	28.22	25.76
M_t^p/d_t^c 100	7.45	89.09	50.47	61.77	87.89	58.17	66.07	76.99	58.66	60.19	59.60	47.47

Excluding 1956 (when P.L. 480 imports were very small), the correlation of these two series is 0.9219.

11. J. Johnston, *Econometric Methods* (New York: McGraw-Hill Book Company, 1960).

12. National Council of Applied Economic Research, *Long-Term Projections of Demand and Supply of Selected Agricultural Commodities: 1960–61 to 1975–76* (New Delhi: NCAER, 1962).

13. *Economic Survey of Asia and the Far East* (Bangkok: ECAFE, 1965), p. 71. (Annual Number)

14. We used the multiplicative logarithmic form of supply and demand functions for ease of solution in the simplified model. Although food aid is additive along the two functions as a constant rather than multiplicative as a relative change, the two forms will not differ significantly in value around equilibrium. If K is defined as the quantity of food aid imported and Ψ is defined as 1.0 plus the fraction K divided by the equilibrium quantity of supply, $cP^\epsilon \Psi$ will not differ significantly from $cP^\epsilon + K$ for adjustments around equilibrium. At prices above equilibrium, $cP^\epsilon \Psi$ is slightly greater than $cP^\epsilon + K$; below equilibrium $cP^\epsilon \Psi$ is slightly less than $cP^\epsilon + K$. Similar logic applies to the demand function.

15. If P.L. 480 commodities are valued below similar domestic products, the income effect will be less than the shift in supply, so it would be appropriate to modify the definition of the demand supply by multiplying Ψ by the ratio of P.L. 480 prices to domestic prices. Redefining; $\Gamma = 1.0 + MPC \ (\Psi - 1.0) \ (P_{\text{P.L. }480}/P_{\text{domestic}})$ is derived from $\Gamma - 1.0 = MPC \ (\Psi - 1.0)$, which implies $\Gamma = 1.0 + MPC \ (\Psi - 1.0)$.

CHAPTER THREE

1. OECD, *Developing World: The Flow of Financial Resources to Less Developed Countries, 1961–65*, Annex 1.

2. Per Pinstrup-Anderson and Luther G. Tweeten, "The Value, Cost and Efficiency of American Food Aid," *Am. J. Agri. Econ.* 53 (Aug. 1971): 431–40.

3. Ibid., p. 438.

4. Charles R. Frank, Jr., William R. Cline, and Thomas Gewecke, "Debt Servicing Problems of Less Developed Countries and Terms of Foreign Aid."

5. Ibid., pp. 37–45.

6. Pinstrup-Anderson and Tweeten, p. 434.

7. Ibid., p. 437.

8. Earl O. Heady, Leo V. Mayer, Howard C. Madsen, *Future Farm Programs*.

9. Ibid., p. 260.

CHAPTER FOUR

1. For a detailed exposition of the problems raised by the counterpart funds, see Alexix E. Lachman, *The Local Currency Proceeds of Foreign Aid.*

2. For the details of the controversy, see Uma K. Srivastava, *Impact of P.L. 480 Aid on India's Money Supply and External Debt Service Obligations.*

3. Such an analysis implicitly assumes (1) that no portion of the additional money supply would be absorbed by an incremental demand for holding of money and (2) that a balanced budget will not necessarily lead to any changes in prices. The Keynesian framework of analysis defines the motives of holding money (a) for speculation, (b) for transactions, and (c) for precautionary purposes. Any one of these motives might lead to a change in the demand for holding money. We also know that the government outlays, even if financed only out of taxes in a balanced budget framework, could lead to a net expansion in demand and a *ceteris paribus* rise in prices, depending on where the outlays go.

4. See Uma K. Srivastava, "Impact of P.L. 480 on Indian Economy"; K. Sundram, "The Relationship between P.L. 480 Transactions Money Supply with Public and Prices: An Analysis," *Indian Econ. Rev.* [N.S.] 5(Apr. 1971): 71–96.

5. P.L. 480 funds were to be transferred from the SBI to the RBI as follows: (1) Rs 12 crores each month from July 1960 to June 1961; (2) Rs 10 crores each month from Nov. 1962 to Mar. 1963; (3) Rs 6 crores each month from Nov. 1963 to Mar. 1964; (4) Rs 8 crores each month from Nov. 1964 to Mar. 1965; and (5) Rs 5 crores in Nov. 1965 and Rs 4 crores each month from Dec. 1965 to Mar. 1966 (compiled from *Reserve Bank of India Bulletins*).

6. It has been found that "P.L. 480 deposits enabled the State Bank of India to divert more funds from government securities to make larger advances than would otherwise have been possible. To the extent State Bank used P.L. 480 to increase its credit ratio, it increased the money supply with the public." See Nilakantha Rath and V. S. Patvardhan, *Impact of Assistance under P.L. 480 on Indian Economy,* Gokhale Institute of Economics and Politics, 1967. Besides, "the old procedure used to overstate the time deposits of the private sector with the banks, as well as bank investments in the government securities, hence overstating the bank credit to government sector and understating the government deposits with the Reserve Bank and the Reserve Bank's holding of rupee securities." See Mohsin Z. Mogri, "Impact of P.L. 480 Counterpart Funds on Money Supply Variations and on Deficit Financing," *Economic Times,* Aug. 22, 1963.

7. "The final disbursement by the USAID from the counterpart funds would demand the monetization of special securities, e.g., the creation of money by the Reserve Bank against the treasury bills, for redeeming the special securities as the cash balance being at the minimum the government will have no funds to redeem the special securities." B. R. Shenoy, "P.L. 480 Counterpart Funds and Inflation," I & II, *Economic Times,* Mar. 27 and 28, 1963.

8. The investment sustained by P.L. 480 commodities has been much more, but this index represents a least amount of noninflationary investment.

9. A. M. Khusro, *A Survey of Monetary Economics in India.*

10. The USAID estimate came up during our discussion with some of the Embassy officials at the Financial Attaché's office in New Delhi in February 1970. We picked up the USAID estimates from our discussion with loan disbursement officials at the USAID Mission in New Delhi. However, the assumptions about the future are our own judgment based on the discussions with the officials.

11. Appendix Table C.5 presents data on national income, imports of commodities and services (M), and the minimum requirements of commodities and services at current as well as constant prices (base 1960–61). The following regression equation uses the data at constant prices to avoid the effects of price fluctuations. While the data on national income are available for the period 1957–58 through 1967–68 at 1960–61 prices, the data of imports and exports at current prices were deflated by their corresponding unit value indices of DGCIS (Director General Commercial Intelligence

and Statistics). As the indices were available with the base $1958 = 100$ for the period 1960–61 through 1967–68 and with base $1952–53 = 100$ for the earlier period, both series were first brought to a common base $(1958 = 100)$ and then the base was shifted to 1960–61. The services component of exports and imports was also deflated by the general price level in the absence of any other reliable indicator. Then each commodity group was deflated with its corresponding unit value to arrive at the estimates of minimum requirements of imports at 1960–61 prices. The estimates of regression equations are as follows:

(1) $\overline{M} = 101.40 + 0.0545Y - 0.2869R \qquad R^2 = 0.694$
$\phantom{(1) \overline{M} = 101.40 +} (2.71) \qquad (-0.38)$

(2) $\overline{M} = -73.46 + 0.0600Y \qquad R^2 = 0.689$
$\phantom{(2) \overline{M} = -73.46 +} (4.46)$

(3) $M = -1430.42 + 0.1189Y + 1.6275R \qquad R^2 = 0.826$
$ (5.29) \qquad (1.55)$

(4) $M = -438.68 + 0.1089Y \qquad R^2 = 0.773$
$ (5.54)$

where $\overline{M}$ = minimum imports in crores of rupees.
$ M$ = total imports in crores of rupees.
$ Y$ = national income in crores of rupees
$ R$ = foreign exchange reserves in crores of rupees.
The value of 8% was taken to lie between the minimum and the maximum (coefficients of Y in equations 2 and 4). Value of t statistics are in parentheses.

12. These elasticity figures are from an unpublished Planning Commission (India) working paper on the projection of food grain demand.

13. Government of India, *Report on Price Policy for Kharif Cereals for the 1971–72 Season* (New Delhi: Ministry of Food and Agriculture, 1971), p. 2.

14. Ralph W. Cummings, Jr., "Long Range Agricultural Adjustment Analysis," *Indian J. Agr. Econ.* 26 (Jan.–Mar. 1971): 1–20; USAID, *Long Range Agricultural Analysis* (New Delhi: USAID, 1969) mimeo.

15. National Council of Applied Economic Research, *Demand and Supply Projections of Food Grains in India—1970–71 to 1985–86.*

16. Ibid., p. 4.

17. S. K. Ray, "Food Grain Demand and Supply—Projections of Regional Imbalances," *Economic and Political Weekly* 6 (June 26, 1971): 10–12.

18. S. K. Ray, "Demand for Food in India, 1968–69 to 1983–84."

19. A. M. Khusro, "Recession, Inflation and Economic Policy," *Economic and Political Weekly* 2 (Oct. 14, 1967): 1857–62.

CHAPTER FIVE

1. Uma K. Srivastava, Robert W. Crown, and Earl O. Heady, "Green Revolution and Farm Income Distribution," *Economic and Political Weekly* 6 (Dec. 25, 1971): A163–A164; Earl O. Heady, "Basic Economic and Welfare Aspects of Farm Technological Advance," *J. Farm Econ.* 22 (May 1949): 293–316.

2. Hiromitsu Kaneda, "Economic Implications of the 'Green Revolution' and Strategy of Agricultural Development in West Pakistan," *Pakistan Development Review* 9 (Summer 1969): 111–43; Clifton R. Wharton, "The Green Revolution: Cornucopia or Pandora's Box?" *Foreign Affairs* 47 (Apr. 1969): 464–76; and Walter P. Falcon, "The Green Revolution, Generation of Problems," *Am. J. Agr. Econ.* 52 (Dec. 1971): 698–772.

3. Ian R. Wills, "Projections of Effects of Modern Inputs on Agricultural Income and Employment in a Community Development Block, Uttar Pradesh, India," *Am. J. Agr. Econ.* 54 (Aug. 1972): 452–60.

4. Uma K. Srivastava and Earl O. Heady, "Technological Change and Relative Factor Shares in Indian Agriculture: An Empirical Analysis," *Am. J. Agr. Econ.* 55:509–15.

5. M. Schluter, "Differential Rates of Adoption on the New Seed Varieties in India: The Problems of Small Farms," Occasional Paper 47, Dept. Agr. Econ., Cornell University, 1971.

6. B. S. Minhas, "Rural Poverty, Land Redistribution, and Development Strategy: Facts and Policy," *Indian Econ. Rev.* [N.S.] 5 (Apr. 1970): 97–128.

7. Pranab K. Bardhan, "On the Minimum Levels of Living and the Rural Poor," *Indian Econ. Rev.* [N.S.] 5 (Apr. 1970): 129–36.

8. Uma Lele, "The Green Revolution: Income Distribution and Nutrition," Occasional Paper 48, Dept. Agr. Econ., Cornell University, 1971.

9. FAO/UN, *Provisional Indicative World Plan for Agricultural Development: Summary and Main Conclusions*, p. 15.

10. Ibid., p. 35.

11. Ibid., p. 37.

12. Ibid., p. 47.

APPENDIX A

1. FAO/UN, *Use of Agricultural Surpluses to Finance Economic Development in Underdeveloped Countries*, p. 9.

2. Theodore J. Goering and Lawrence Witt, *United States Agricultural Surpluses in Colombia*.

3. Haven D. Umstott, *Public Law 480 and Other Economic Assistance to United Arab Republic (Egypt)*, USDA, ERS Foreign Rept. 83, June 1964.

4. Parameters used for the U.A.R. were: $p = 3.0, g = 2.67, n = 0.7; d = p + gn = 4.87$.

5. Resat Aktan, *Analysis and Assessment of the Economic Effects of Public Law 480 Title I Program, Turkey*.

6. Elmer L. Menzie, Lawrence W. Witt, Carl K. Eicher, and Jimmye S. Hillman, *Policy for United States Agricultural Export Surplus Disposal*.

7. Nilakantha Rath and V. S. Patvardhan, *Impact of Assistance under P.L. 480 on Indian Economy*.

APPENDIX B

1. Government of India, *Report of the Expert Group on Monetary Impact of P.L. 480 Transactions*.

BIBLIOGRAPHY

Adams, Dale, et al., *Public Law 480 and Colombia's Economic Development* (Medillin, Colombia: Facultad de Agronomia E. Instituto Forestall Universidad Nacional de Colombia and Michigan State University, 1964).

Aktan, Resat, *Analysis and Assessment of the Economic Effects of Public Law 480 Title 1 Program, Turkey* (Ankara: University of Ankara, 1964).

Arrow, K. J., Chenery, H., Minhas, B. S., and Solow, R., "Capital-Labor Substitution and Economic Efficiency," *Rev. Economics and Statistics* 43 (Aug. 1961): 225–50.

Asher, Robert E., *Grants, Loans and Local Currencies: Their Role in Foreign Aid.* (Washington, D.C.: Brookings Institution, 1962).

Bardhan, P. K., "On the Minimum Levels of Living and the Rural Poor," *Indian Econ. Rev.* [N.S.] 5 (Apr. 1970): 129–36.

———, "Size, Productivity and Returns to Scale: An Analysis of Farm Level Data in Indian Agriculture," paper presented to conference at Food Research Institute, Stanford University, Dec. 1971.

Beringer, Christopher, and Ahmad, Irshad, *The Use of Agricultural Surplus Commodities for Economic Development in Pakistan* (Karachi: Institute of Development Economics, 1964).

Bhagwati, Jagdish N., and Desai, Padma, *India, Planning for Industrialization: Industrialization and Trade Policies Since 1951* (London: Oxford University Press, 1970).

Billings, Martin H., and Singh, Arjan, "Agriculture and Technological Change in Maharastra, 1968–84," Agr. Econ. Div., USAID, New Delhi, Apr. 1970, mimeo.

Brown, Murray, *On the Theory of Technological Change* (Cambridge: Cambridge University Press, 1966).

FAO/UN. *The Linking of Food Aid with Other Aid* (Rome: FAO, 1964).

———, *Provisional Indicative World Plan for Agricultural Development: Summary and Main Conclusions* (Rome: FAO, 1970).

———, *Use of Agricultural Surpluses to Finance Economic Development in Underdeveloped Countries,* Commodity Policy Series No. 6 (Rome: FAO, 1966).

Fisher, Franklin M., "A Theoretical Analysis of the Impact of Food Surplus Disposal on Agricultural Production in Recipient Countries," *J. Farm Econ.* 45 (Nov. 1963): 863–75.

Frank, Charles R., Jr., Cline, William R., and Gewecke, Thomas, "Debt Servicing Problems of Less Developed Countries and Terms of Foreign Aid: With Special Reference to United States Policy" (Washington, D.C.: USAID, 1968), mimeo.

Ginor, Fanny, *Use of Agricultural Surpluses, Analysis and Assessment of the Economic Effects of the U.S. Public Law 480 Title 1 Program in Israel* (Jerusalem: Research Department, Bank of Israel, 1963).

Goering, Theodore J., and Witt, Lawrence, *United States Agricultural Surpluses in Colombia, A Review of P.L. 480,* Tech. Bull. 289 (East Lansing: Michigan State University, 1963).

Goreux, L. M., "Income and Food Consumption," *FAO Monthly Bull.* 9 (Oct. 1960): 1–13.

Government of India, *Report of the Study Team on Fair Price Shops, Department of Food* (New Delhi: GOI Press, 1966).

———, *Report of the Expert Group on Monetary Impact of P.L. 480 Transactions* (New Delhi: GOI Press, 1960).

Heady, Earl O., Mayer, Leo V., and Madsen, Howard C., *Future Farm Programs: Comparative Costs and Consequences* (Ames: Iowa State University Press, 1972).

Houthakkar, Hendrik S., "An International Comparison of Household Expenditure Patterns, Commemorating the Centenary of Engel's Law," *Econometrica* 25 (Oct. 1957): 532–51.

Johnston, Bruce F., and Cownie, John, "The Seed-Fertilizer Revolution and Labor Force Absorption," *Am. Econ. Rev.* 59 (Sept. 1969): 582–96.

Kaneda, Hiromitsu, "Economic Implications of the 'Green Revolution' and Strategy of Agricultural Development in West Pakistan," *Pakistan Development Rev.* 9 (Summer 1969): 111–43.

Kahn, Alfred E., "Agricultural Aid and Economic Development, the Case of Israel," *Quart. J. Econ.* 76 (Nov. 1962): 568–91.

Khatkhate, Deena R., "Some Notes on the Real Effects of Foreign Surplus Disposal in Underdeveloped Economies," *Quart. J. Econ.* 76 (May 1962): 186–96.

Khusro, A. M., "A Survey of Monetary Economics in India" (New Delhi: Institute of Economic Growth, 1971), mimeo.

Lachman, Alexix E., *The Local Currency Proceeds of Foreign Aid* (Paris: OECD, 1968).

Mann, Jitendar S., "The Impact of Public Law 480 Imports on Prices and Domestic Supply of Cereals in India," *J. Farm Econ.* 49 (Feb. 1967): 131–46.

Mellor, John W., *The Economics of Agricultural Development* (Ithaca: Cornell University Press, 1966).

Menzie, Elmer L., Witt, Lawrence W., Eicher, Carl K., and Hillman, Jimmye S., *Policy for United States Agricultural Export Surplus Disposal*, Ariz. Agr. Exp. Sta. Tech. Bull. 150, 1962.

Narain, Dharam, and Rao, V. K. R. V., *Foreign Aid and India's Economic Development,* Occasional Paper No. 3 (New Delhi: Institute of Economic Growth, 1963).

National Council of Applied Economic Research (in cooperation with the Center for Agricultural and Economic Development). *Demand and Supply Projections of Food Grains for India: 1970–71 to 1985–86* Dev. Ser. Rept. 3 (Ames: CAED, 1970).

OECD, *Developing World—The Flow of Financial Resources to Less Developed Countries, 1962–68* (Paris: OECD, 1970).

Pak, Ki Hyuk, and Hau, Kee Chun, *An Analysis of Food Consumption in the Republic of Korea* (Seoul: Honsei University, 1969).

Pincus, John, *Economic Aid and International Cost Sharing* (Baltimore: Johns Hopkins Press, 1965).

Pinstrup-Anderson, Per, "The Role of Food, Feed, and Fiber in Foreign Economic Assistance: Value, Cost, and Efficiency," Ph.D. thesis (Stillwater: Oklahoma State University, 1959).

Pinstrup-Anderson, Per, and Tweeten, Luther G., "The Value, Cost and Efficiency of American Food Aid," *Am. J. Agr. Econ.* 53 (Aug. 1971: 431–40.

Rath, Nilakantha, and Patvardhan, V. S., *Impact of Assistance under P.L. 480 on Indian Economy,* Gokhale Institute of Economics and Politics (Poona: Asia Publishing House, 1967).

Ray, S. K., "Demand for Food in India, 1968–69 to 1983–84" (New Delhi: USAID, 1969), mimeo.

————, "Food Grain Demand and Supply—Projection of Regional Imbalances," *Economic and Political Weekly* 6 (June 26, 1971): 10–12.

Rogers, Keith D., "Theory and Application of Food Aid in Economic Development," Ph.D. thesis (Ames: Iowa State University, 1971).

Rogers, Keith D., Srivastava, Uma K., and Heady, Earl O., "Modified Price, Production and Income Impacts of Food Aid under Market Differentiated Distribution," *Am. J. Agr. Econ.* 54 (May 1972): 201–8.

Schultz, Theodore W., *Transforming Traditional Agriculture* (New Haven: Yale University Press, 1964).

————, "Value of U.S. Farm Surpluses to Underdeveloped Countries," *J. Farm Econ.* 42(Dec. 1960): 1019–30.

Sharma, J. S., "Feeding India's Population in 1980—A Quantitative Assessment," Resource Papers, National Food Congress, Ministry of Food and Agriculture, New Delhi, May 1970, pp. 1–12.

Srivastava, Uma K., "The Impact of Public Law 480 Imports on Prices and Domestic Supply of Cereals in India: Comment," *Am. J. Agr. Econ.* 50 (Feb. 1968): 143–45.

————, "Impact of P.L. 480 on Indian Economy," Ph.D. thesis (Lucknow: Lucknow University, India, 1969).

————, *Impact of P.L. 480 Aid on India's Money Supply and External Debt Service Obligations: A Look Ahead* (Ames: CARD Rept. 44, 1972).

Srivastava, U. K., Crown, Robert W., and Heady, Earl O., "Green Revolution and Farm Income Distribution," *Economic and Political Weekly* 6 (Dec. 25, 1971): A163–A172.

Srivastava, U. K., and Heady, Earl O., "Technological Change and Relative Factor Shares in Indian Agriculture: An Empirical Analysis," *Am. J. Agr. Econ.* 55:509–15, 1972.

Stevens, Robert D., *Elasticity of Food Consumption Associated with Changes in Income in Developing Countries,* Foreign Agr. Econ. Rept. 23 (Washington: USDA, 1965).

Sundaram, K., "The Relationship between P.L. 480 Transactions, Money Supply with Public and Prices: An Analysis," *Indian Econ. Rev.* [N.S.] 5 (Apr. 1970):71–96.

Thorbecke, E., and Stoutjesdijk, E., *Employment and Output—A Methodology Applied to Peru and Guatemala,* Development Center Studies, Employment Ser. 2 (Paris: OECD, 1971).

Turnham, David, *The Employment Problems in Less Developed Countries—A Review of Evidence,* Development Center Studies (Paris: OECD, 1970).

U.S. Congress, *Food for Peace,* House Doc. No. 104–91/1 (Washington, D.C.: GPO, 1969).

Foreign Affairs 47 (Apr. 1969): 464–76.

Wharton, Clifton R., "The Green Revolution: Cornucopia or Pandora's Box?"

Wills, Ian R., "Projections of Effects of Modern Inputs on Agricultural Income and Employment in a Community Development Block, Uttar Pradesh, India," *Am. J. Agr. Econ.* 54 (Aug. 1972): 452–60.

Witt, Lawrence, and Eicher, Carl, *The Effects of United States Agricultural Surplus Disposal Program on the Recipient Countries* (East Lansing: Michigan State University, 1964).

INDEX

Ad hocs, 90, 93
Aggregate demand for food, 14

Barter program, 8, 11

CCC. *See* Commodity Credit Corporation
Closed economy, 15
Colombia, Goering and Witt study of P.L. 480 impact on economy, 124–26
Commercial exports, U.S., 12–13
Commercial import equation, 43–44, 47
Commodity Credit Corporation, 4–5, 84, 85, 119
Commodity mix, needed changes, 117, 119
Cooley funds and loans, 5, 7, 89, 90, 93, 94, 96, 98, 101
Cooperative for American Relief Everywhere (CARE), 5
Counterpart funds
  defined, 87
  inflationary implications, 87–89
  minimum multiplier effect, 111–12
  necessary and sufficiency conditions, 88
  P.L. 480 net support (India), 96, 98

DAC. *See* Development Assistance Committee
Debt services charges, LDCs, 76, 79, 120, 121
  India, 80–81
Delay multiplier, 49–50
Derived food demand, 27, 30, 34, 35
Development Assistence Committee (DAC), 64
  aid terms, 64–66
Development, project approach
  model, 54–61
  wages, 24–25, 28, 34–35
Differentiated market, need for, 63
Dollar-repayable food aid, 72, 74, 76
  aid component, 74, 76, 81
  alternative price levels, 81–86
Donation programs, 126

Elasticity, defined, 24
Employment increase, as result of food aid, 23, 31
Engel curve, 23
Engel's law, 18, 19
Equations, impact of P.L. 480 cereals shipments, 41–45, 47
Extended loan contracts, repayment schedule, 67–70

Fair-price shop distribution (India), 40, 42, 51, 53, 61, 93, 94, 122, 131, 132

Food aid
  conclusions, 17–18, 35–36, 86, 113
  development projects, 116–17
  feed grains, 119
  and financing of development projects, 23–25, 27–28, 30–32, 34–35
  high income recipients, 31–32, 34–35
  low income recipients, 22–25, 27–28
  medium income recipients, 28, 30–31
  mutuality of interests involved, 119–21
  policy guidelines, 121–22
  price disincentive effects on agricultural production, 37–39
  shortcomings, 130
Food aid programs
  commodity impact, 133
  local currency impact, 133
  studies and conclusions, 133–34
Food consumption
  India, 19, 20
  Korea, 20
Food demand (higher income), 32
Food distribution programs, criticisms, 115–16
Food gap, 15
Food grain supply (India), Ray's projections, 111
Foreign exchange constraint, 80
Foreign exchange gap, 16, 17

Gokhale Institute, study of India, 131–32
Grant element, dollar sales, 70–72, 74, 76
  dollar repayable aid formula, 72, 74
  formula, 71–72
Grantlike aid, 64, 65, 80
Green Revolution, 37, 113–16

High income recipients, food aid, 31–32, 34–35

Imports, resulting from food aid, 30, 32, 34, 35
Income elasticity of food demand, 21
Income equation, 43, 46–47
Income levels, effect on food demand, 21–25, 27–28, 30–32, 34–35
Income multiplier, defined, 27
India
  FAO study, use of surplus commodities, 123–24
  Gokhale Institute study, 131–32
  P.L. 480 operations, 135–38, 140–43
  allocation of funds, 135–38
  budget entries for P.L. 480, 143
  transactions, 138, 140–43
Interagency Staff Committee (ISC), 6–7
International aid, grants and loans, 64–66

LIBRARY OF DAVIDSON COLLEGE

Books on regular loan may be checked out for **two weeks**. Books must be presented at the Circulation Desk in order to be renewed.

A fine is charged after date due.

Special books are subject to special regulations at the discretion of library staff.